THE SATURDAY EVENING PEARLS

Other *Pearls Before Swine* Collections

Macho Macho Animals
The Sopratos
Da Brudderhood of Zeeba Zeeba Eata
The Ratvolution Will Not Be Televised
Nighthogs
This Little Piggy Stayed Home
BLTs Taste So Darn Good

Treasuries

The Crass Menagerie
Lions and Tigers and Crocs, Oh My!
Sgt. Piggy's Lonely Hearts Club Comic

Gift Book

Da Crockydile Book o' Frendsheep

THE SATURDAY EVENING PEARLS

A *Pearls Before Swine* Collection

by Stephan Pastis

Andrews McMeel Publishing, LLC

Kansas City

Pearls Before Swine is distributed internationally by United Feature Syndicate.

For information, write Andrews McMeel Publishing, LLC, an Andrews McMeel Universal company, 1130 Walnut Street, Kansas City, Missouri 64106.

09 10 11 12 13 BBG 10 9 8 7 6 5 4 3 2 1

ISBN-13: 978-0-7407-7391-4
ISBN-10: 0-7407-7391-7

Library of Congress Control Number: 2008936161

www.andrewsmcmeel.com

Pearls Before Swine can be viewed on the Internet at
www.comics.com/pearls_before_swine.

These strips appeared in newspapers from May 14, 2007, to February 16, 2008.

For all my teachers at Carver Elementary School,
Huntington Junior High, and San Marino High School,
who put up with me for far too little money.

Introduction

Syndicated cartoonists are in an odd situation.

On the one hand, they draw characters that can be recognized by millions of people. On the other hand, they themselves are virtually unknown.

Let me put it another way. How many syndicated cartoonists could you recognize if you saw them walking down the street?

The answer for most people is probably none.

Think about that for a second. Just yesterday, you might have been at a Burger King or Dunkin' Donuts standing behind Gary Larson or Bill Watterson, and you wouldn't have known it.

This creates some bizarre situations. For example, I've been at a coffee shop watching the guy sitting next to me reading my strip. But he has no idea who I am. He's just wondering why the strange guy with the poorly trimmed goatee is staring at him.

I think the only times I've ever been recognized by anyone were when I've had to give them my name (e.g., making reservations, handing someone my credit card, etc.), but even those occurrences are relatively few.

So syndicated cartoonists are a little like the wizard guy in *The Wizard of Oz*. Short, little fat men hiding behind a curtain. Only there's no Toto to pull it open. (Which is probably a good thing, because I've seen most syndicated cartoonists and believe me, you don't want that curtain open.)

Nevertheless, for reasons only a therapist could understand, I tried to rectify this strange anonymity by putting my own photo on the front cover of my last treasury, *The Crass Menagerie*. It takes a special kind of blinding, megalomaniacal idiocy to put your own photo on the cover of a comic strip compilation book. I have that.

But beyond just the issue of knowing what a cartoonist looks like is the issue of knowing who a cartoonist really is.

A few, like Scott Adams and Jim Borgman, keep blogs. Some of the giants, like Charles Schulz and George Herriman, have biographies written about them. But for all the other cartoonists, who they are remains a bit of a mystery.

I think this is because the majority of cartoonists are known only through the newspaper interviews they give, and those tend to rehash the same questions over and over (e.g., Which character do you identify with most? Did you draw as a kid? Where do you get your ideas?, etc.). Read one and for the most part, you've read them all. As a result, you never really learn what radio host Paul Harvey would call "the rest of the story."

So just as I addressed the physical anonymity issue by including my photo on the *Menagerie* cover (thereby jeopardizing sales), I'm now going to risk even more by telling everyone more about me personally.

(I should add here that my longtime best friend, Emilio, believes this is a big mistake. I am, to use his term, a "total jackass," and the less people know about me the better. The problem is that he, too, is a "total jackass," and thus I must discount everything he says.)

So, without further delay, I boldly present:

Nineteen Facts I've Always Wanted to Reveal about Myself But Have Never Gotten the Chance Because Nobody Asked

Fact No. 1
I am afraid of dogs. Not all dogs. Just the ones that bark.

Fact No. 2
I am superstitious. I will not walk onto the handicapped symbols that are painted on the handicap spots in a parking lot.

Fact No. 3
Another superstition: When I am sleeping on my stomach, and my head is facing toward one side, I will not let the opposite shoulder be uncovered by the blanket.

Fact No. 4
I once stepped out of my hotel room at the Millennium Biltmore Hotel in Los Angeles and ran into Muhammad Ali, who was walking down the hall. Like the guy at the coffee shop, he did not know me.

Fact No. 5
I am Icarian, meaning that my family is from a tiny island in Greece called Ikaria. It is named for Icarus, the character in Greek mythology who ambitiously flew too close to the sun and died. If I am lucky, this will not be a metaphor for my career.

Fact No. 6
The first job I ever had was working at my uncle's restaurant in South Pasadena, California. I made the salads, took the chickens off the rotisserie, and spoke in Spanish to Juan, the dishwasher. When things were slow, I put horseradish in Juan's orange juice.

Fact No. 7
When I was eight, I was ejected from a Little League game for disputing a third strike call and throwing my batting helmet. When my dad showed up halfway into the game, he looked for me in the dugout but could not find me. I think he knew something was wrong when I waved to him from the bleachers.

Fact No. 8
I am convinced it's good luck when I look at the clock and it says, "11:11."

Fact No. 9
None of my neighbors like me. In fact, I think they hate me. As far as I'm concerned, they have no valid basis for hating me, as I've steadfastly refused to talk to them.

Fact No. 10
I am allergic to cats. If a friend buys a cat, I have to stop going to their house.

Fact No. 11
Many of my friends and neighbors have started buying cats.

Fact No. 12
I was once on national television dancing on *Dick Clark's New Year's Rockin' Eve*.

Fact No. 13
I will never reveal another fact as embarrassing as Fact No. 12.

Fact No. 14
I once called my cousin to come over and play, then climbed up on my roof and waited for him with a slingshot and acorns. When he arrived, I hit him with so many acorns, he turned around on his little bicycle and rode home.

Fact No. 15
I once telephoned that same cousin and in a deep voice told him that I was the superintendent of schools and was transferring him to another school due to poor grades (knowing full well that he did in fact have poor grades). I knew he fell for it when he started to cry.

Fact No. 16
Upon graduating from junior high school, my fellow eighth graders voted me "Most Obnoxious." Upon graduating from high school, my fellow twelfth graders voted me "Most Obnoxious" again. This made me the only student in the history of the San Marino school system to win the award in both years of eligibility. Had my college given out such an award, I think I could have scored a three-peat.

Fact No. 17
When I drank too much in college, I would sometimes run back to my apartment as fast as I could with my arms extended out at my sides because it made me think I could fly.

Fact No. 18
I once ran for City Council in my hometown of Albany, California, but then refused to give interviews, causing the local paper to term me "Mystery Candidate Pastis." My contrarian strategy did not pay off. I lost in a landslide.

Fact No. 19
I met my wife at a bar in Berkeley. She was there with a few of her friends. I asked her friends what her name was and they said it was Staci. So I walked up to her and said, "I love you, Staci," making me the only guy I know whose first words to his wife were, "I love you."

And there you have . . . the rest of the story.

Stephan Pastis
March 2009

HELLO, GOD. YOU DON'T KNOW ME... I'M RAT.
YOU SAY ASK AND IT SHALL BE GIVEN...
SO GIVE ME ONE BILLION DOLLARS AND THE LOOKS TO ATTRACT RACHEL McADAMS.
5/14
SHAKE SHAKE SHAKE
MY FAITH IS WANING.

Hulloooooo, leetle rat... How is you?
WHY DO YOU HAVE A PAIR OF BAGGY JEANS PULLED UP TO YOUR NECK?

5/15
Baggy jeans cool. Me a rebel. Girls love.
DUDE, YOU LOOK RIDICULOUS...GUYS WEAR THEIR JEANS REAL LOW NOW.

OH LAAAAADIES!
I DON'T WANT TO KNOW... I DON'T WANT TO KNOW.

CAN I HELP YOU?
HI. WE'RE THE DEATHS. WE JUST MOVED IN NEXT DOOR... JUST WANTED TO SAY HIYA.
ARF ARF

HEEEY. WELCOME, WELCOME...Y'KNOW, IF YOU HAVE ANY QUESTIONS OR CONCERNS, FEEL FREE TO ASK.
WELL, WE DO HAVE ONE.
WHAT'S THAT?

5/16
HOW SAFE IS THE NEIGHBORHOOD?

RAT AND PIG GET NEW NEIGHBORS, THE DEATHS.
GOSH, MR. DEATH, I SURE APPRECIATE YOUR SHOWING ME YOUR NEW HOUSE...
OH, NO PROBLEM, PIG... BUT CALL ME 'DEATH.'
OH.. OKAY. I WILL... HEY, EXCUSE ME FOR A MINUTE...
RIIIIING RIIIIING
HELLO?
PIG, IT'S ME, RAT.. YOU'RE S'POSED TO BE MOWING THE LAWN. WHERE ARE YOU?
I'M AT DEATH'S DOOR.
NICE TRY.

SEE YA, RAT.
YOU GOING SWIMMING?

NO. WHY?
BECAUSE PEOPLE ONLY WEAR INFLATABLE RAFTS WHEN THEY'RE GOING SWIMMING.

I HAVE SO MUCH TROUBLE ACCESSORIZING.

WHY MUST LIFE BE FILLED WITH PAIN? WHY MUST IT FOLLOW YOU ALL YOUR DAYS AND OVERTAKE YOU WITH SUCH REGULARITY?

YEAH, WHY CAN'T WE BE FOLLOWED BY A BIG BUCKET OF 'FIG NEWTONS' INSTEAD? THEY'RE SO TASTY AND THEY BRING YOU SUCH JOY.

THERE'S THAT PAIN AGAIN.
AND SPEAKING OF REGULARITY...

DAD, WILL YOU PLEASE READ ME ONE OF MY 'SESAME STREET' BOOKS? THEY'RE MY FAVORITE.
Sure ting, sweetie...

"Oscar was grouchy. Ernie and Bert had borrowed hees baskeetball and had not returned eet.

'Geeve me back my baskeetball,' said Oscar. 'We can't find eet,' said Ernie.

'But dat's my favorite baskeet-ball,' said Oscar. 'I guess dis ees an important lesson,' said Ernie, 'If you borrow someone's tings, you need to take good care of dem.'"

Unsateesfied, Oscar tear off Ernie's head.

5/20

PLEASE DON'T MAKE UP YOUR OWN ENDINGS, DAD.
Ernie have to pay price, son.

HEY, RAT... I'D LIKE YOU TO MEET MY FRIEND, LEON THE CHAMELEON.
SOME CHAMELEON.. I CAN SEE HIM RIGHT THERE ON THE KITCHEN COUNTER.

WHAT'S WRONG WITH THAT?
THOSE THINGS ARE SUPPOSED TO BLEND IN WITH THEIR SURROUNDINGS.
5/21

OKAY. THAT'S IMPRESSIVE.

OHHHHHH MAN... I'M SO DOWN TODAY.
AWW..DON'T WORRY, L'IL BUDDY... THINGS WILL GET BETTER.

REALLY?
REALLY.

THEN THEY'LL GET WORSE AGAIN.
5/22

OHHHHHHHHH
REALISTS NEVER DO MAKE GOOD COMFORTERS.

WE NEED MONEY. GO INVENT SOMETHING.

5/23

CHEESE SNEAKERS...FOR THE ATHLETE WHO NEEDS A LITTLE SNACK.
OHH, IF MY HIGH SCHOOL GUIDANCE COUNSELOR COULD SEE ME NOW.

ONE OF THE CROCS GOT A JOB. HIS EMPLOYER SAID HE HAD A NICE SMILE.

WHAT KIND OF AN EMPLOYER IS WILLING TO HIRE A TOTAL MORON JUST BECAUSE THEY HAVE A NICE SMILE?
5/24

Baby cheemp born at zoo. Feelm at eleven.
CHANNEL 4
Your local news

...SO IF YOU'RE GONNA BE OUT, BE SURE TO TAKE ALONG A RAINCOAT. IT'LL BE A WET ONE, DAN!
WELL, SO MUCH FOR MY WIFE MAKING ME MOW THE LAWN THIS WEEKEND, HUH, JANE?
Your local

HA HA HA HA HA HA HA HA HA HA HA HA HA HA HA HA HAHA
Ha ha ha ha ha ha ha ha ha ha
HAHAHA HA HA HAHAHA HAHAHA
Your local

DO YOU SUPPOSE LOCAL NEWS MAKES MORE SENSE IF YOU'RE LOBOTOMIZED?
HAHAHA HAHAHA I *LOVE* THESE GUYS!
5/25

HEY, ZEBRA, WHAT'S THE MATTER WITH YOU?
IT'S MY NEIGHBORS, THE CROCS... I CAN'T TAKE THEM ANYMORE. I'M THINKING OF HIRING YOUR GUARD DUCK TO TAKE 'EM OUT.
5/26

DINNER AND A MOVIE?

PERHAPS I'LL KEEP YOU OUT OF THIS.

R.E.M.
1987 Tour
CLICK

BUH DADADUHH
BUH DADA DUH
BUH DADA DUHH
BUHDADADUH DAA

THAT'S GREAT IT DUHDA
DADADUHDADUHDA
DUHDA DADADUH DA
DADADADADUHHHHH

DADUBADUHBADAA
DADADUH BADUH
DADADUH DA DA DA
BADDADADDADADUH

BUHDADADADADA
DADADADUHDA
DABADADABA
BABAH
DAH

BADADADADUHDADUH
DABADADADUHDADUH
DADADADADADADADA

DADADADADADADADA
DUHDUHDUHDUH
DUH...

LEONARD BERNSTEIN!!

GREATEST... SONG... EVER.
...AND WE ONLY KNOW TWO WORDS.

WHAT'S THE MATTER WITH YOU?
EVERYTHING'S BEEN GOING WRONG FOR ME LATELY.

WELL, YOU KNOW THE OLD SAYING, "IF LIFE HANDS YOU LEMONS..."

"HURL THEM AT THE @##@!☆@ WHO GAVE THEM TO YOU!"

NO.
SHOVE 'EM DOWN HIS THROAT?
PUSH 'EM UP HIS NOSE?
OH, C'MON... I GOTTA BE CLOSE.

PIGITA... YOU'RE A GOOD GIRLFRIEND, BUT SOMETIMES YOU'RE A LITTLE MOODY.
I'M SORRY, PIGGY WIGGY.

YOU DON'T HAVE TO BE SORRY.
I'LL BE SORRY IF I WANT TO BE SORRY.

BOOT

SIGH

I JUST WROTE A BOOK OF HUMOROUS STORIES. IT'S COMEDY GOLD.
HAVE YOU SHOWN IT TO ANYONE?

YES, I SHOWED IT TO SOME OF THE CUSTOMERS AT THE CAFE. THEY WERE FALLING OUT OF THEIR CHAIRS.
SO THEY LIKED IT?

NO, WHICH IS WHY I WAS PUSHING THEM OFF OF THEIR CHAIRS.

NEVER MIND.
HUMORLESS MORONS.

I'M GETTING NEW NEXT DOOR NEIGHBORS TODAY.
THE CROCS ARE LEAVING?

NO, IT'S THE OLD COUPLE ON THE OTHER SIDE OF ME...THEY'RE MOVING OUT...I JUST HOPE THE NEW NEIGHBORS ARE FRIENDLY.

DIBS ON THE STRIPED ONE.

DING DONG DING DONG

AAAAHHHHHH

I TOLD YOU WE SHOULD HAVE GONE WITH THE FRUIT BASKET.

WHAT NOW, RAT?
I AM GIGANTOBRAIN, MAN OF INFINITE WISDOM...MAN WHO KNOWS EVERYTHING... ASK ME ANYTHING... ANYTHING.
ZZZT! ZZZT! ZZZT! ZZZT!

WHY ARE THE PEOPLE WHO GO TO NUDE BEACHES THE ONLY PEOPLE YOU DON'T WANT TO SEE NUDE?
ZZZT! ZZZT! ZZZT! ZZZT!

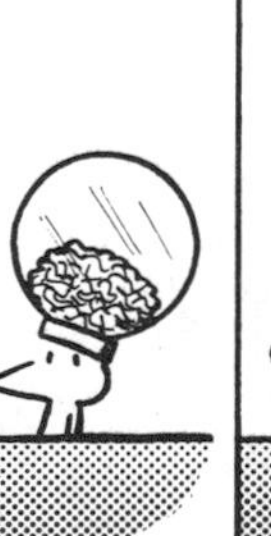

I HAVE MY LIMITATIONS, YOU KNOW.

Dear Zebra,
We are your new neighbors, Max and Zach.
6/3

Do not fear us.
We will not hunt you.
We will not kill you.

Why is that, you ask?

Because as any casual "Animal Planet" viewer can tell you, it's the *female* lions that do the hunting and killing.

We just devour your remains.

Don't take it personal.

DIDN'T YOUR GUARD DUCK BECOME MAYOR OF THE TOWN IN A BIG COUP LAST NOVEMBER?
YEAH. WHY?

IT SAYS HERE THAT NONE OF THE CITY'S BUSINESS IS GETTING DONE.
WELL I'M SURE HE MUST BE DOING SOMETHING.

NOT BIG ENOUGH.
CITY HALL

GOOD MORNING, MR. MAYOR.
GOOD MORNING, MISS CITY CLERK.. HOW ARE THINGS?

NOT SO GOOD, SIR... THE CITY COUNCIL WANTS TO WIPE OUT SOME OF THE EMERGENCY MEASURES YOU ENACTED.
FINE. ELIMINATE THEM.

THE LAWS?
THE CITY COUNCIL.

SIR...
HERE. HIDE THIS IN YOUR SWEATER.

Duuude... Good news... The wife killed that big, fat antelope on 3rd Street.... We've got enough food for a week... High five, bro, you're safe.

SHE KILLED GEORGE? WE'VE BEEN CLOSE FRIENDS FOR SIXTEEN YEARS!.. HE WAS LIKE A BROTHER TO ME!

If you want, we can skip the high five.

DUDE, WHAT ARE YOU DOING? "THE REAL WORLD" IS ON.
NONE OF OUR USUAL CHANNELS ARE COMING IN. ALL I CAN GET IS THIS SPECIAL CALLED "THE GLORY OF WATERFOWL."

WHAT KIND OF MORON NIXES "THE REAL WORLD" FOR THIS?!!

DUCK PROPAGANDA: THE KEY TO GOOD GOVERNANCE.
MAYOR

Duuude... Bad news... The wife spotted you coming home last night. You were wearing a fanny pack. You're doomed.

WHY AM I DOOMED?
Fanny packs show weakness. It's just one of those unspoken rules.

BUT I GOT IT DURING A 'RICK STEVES' PBS PLEDGE BREAK.
Oooooh. That didn't help.

THE FOOD IN THIS PLACE IS REALLY GOING DOWNHILL.
WELL, NEEDLESS TO SAY....

NEEDLESS TO SAY WHAT?
IT WAS NEEDLESS TO SAY.

PLEASE GO AWAY.
HEY, I'M NOT GONNA SAY IT IF IT'S NEEDLESS.

HELLO, SIR... HAVE YOU DECIDED ON WHAT YOU'D LIKE THIS EVENING?
What you got, Meester Bow Tie Man?
MENU

WELL, IF YOU'LL JUST LOOK AT THE MENU, SIR, YOU'LL SEE SOME WONDERFUL FISH—
OH PEEESE. Fish for loozers. Shut mouf.
MENU

UH...... ...SIR, THERE'S REALLY NO NEED TO—
RED MEET RED MEET RED MEET

FINE.. FINE.. SIR... IF YOU'LL JUST SIT BACK DOWN AND TELL ME WHAT KIND OF MEAT YOU'D LIKE, I CAN—

Dis guy.

...AGAIN, SIR, WE CAN'T KILL OTHER CUSTOMERS.
Ohhhhhh.. So you have attitude probbum too, huh?
CHECK, PLEASE.

HEY, ZEBRA... WANT TO COME OVER AND WATCH 'DESPERATE HOUSEWIVES' WITH ME?
I'D LOVE TO, PIG, BUT NIGHTTIME IS WHEN THE WIVES OF THE LIONS NEXT DOOR DO THEIR HUNTING.
Cheese Poofs

WELL, YOU CAN'T STAY HOME EVERY NIGHT, ZEBRA.
I KNOW.. AND I REALLY WANT TO COME OVER. OHH, I DON'T KNOW WHAT TO DO...

Go for it.
Seize the day.

Hermit.
Loner.

GOOD MORNING, MR. MAYOR.
GOOD MORNING, MR. CITY ATTORNEY...LISTEN, I'D LIKE YOU TO START SPYING ON OUR ENEMIES... WIRETAP THEIR OFFICES... THAT SORTA THING.
MAYOR

SIR, I DON'T KNOW IF THAT'S THE BEST THING TO—
PLEASE. I KNOW HOW TO GOVERN. I BOUGHT A BOOK ON IT. I'M DOING WHATEVER THIS GUY DID.
MAYOR

SIR, THAT'S 'ALL THE PRESIDENT'S MEN.'
NOW, WHAT IS THIS 'WATERGATE HOTEL' AND WHY DO I NEED TO BREAK INTO IT?
MAYOR

MAYOR, THERE'S BEEN A RUMOR THAT YOU'VE PLACED RECORDING DEVICES THROUGHOUT OUR OFFICES.

WHY THAT'S ABSURD!
SLAM

WHY THAT'S ABSURD!

MUST BE AN ECHO.

Duuude...Bad news... The wife saw you eating nonfat blueberry yogurt. You may be hosed.
WHAT'S WRONG WITH EATING YOGURT?

Uh...Not a guy food, bro... Now she thinks you're weak. An easy mark. And if......... Uhh, dude...What's that sticker on your book say?

'OPRAH'S BOOK CLUB.' WHY?
Oh, dear God.

...YEAH, DUDE, IT'S ME...I'M AT THE MOVIES...HUH?... YEAH. SWEET...NO...PRETTY DUMB... HUH?..YOU CUT OUT...YEAH... WANNA HOOK UP AFTER OR—

WHAM!

IT SURE BEATS ASKING POLITELY.

WHERE WERE YOU THIS MORNING?
I WAS TALKING TO ANDY, THAT LITTLE DOG ACROSS THE STREET... BOY, DOES HE HAVE BIG PLANS... HE'S GONNA BACKPACK THROUGH ITALY, SAFARI IN KENYA AND SIP TEA IN SHANGHAI.

DUDE...IT'S ONE THING TO HAVE DREAMS... IT'S ANOTHER TO BE DELUSIONAL.
WHAT'S SO DELUSIONAL ABOUT WANTING TO SEE THE WORLD?

WHAT ARE YOU DOING, RAT?
I'M COMING TO GRIPS WITH MY OWN TRANSIENCE BY DRAWING IN THE SAND.

AS SOON AS I FINISH, A WAVE WIPES IT OUT.

THIS HELPS ME COME TO TERMS WITH MY OWN MORTALITY, BECAUSE NO MATTER WHAT I DO...

...I SEE IT WILL ALL BE FORGOTTEN IN TIME.

AND YOU'RE OKAY WITH THAT?
OF COURSE I AM...IT'S THE NATURE OF LIFE... YOU HAVE TO BE OKAY WITH IT.

WELL, GOOD FOR YOU.
THANK YOU.

DUDE, CHECK OUT THIS JOB LISTING..."FLOOR MANAGER, LARGE PARTY SUPPLY STORE... TWENTY-FIVE DOLLARS AN HOUR..INTERVIEWS BEING HELD TODAY..."
6/18

HOLY SMOKES..."INCLUDES HEALTH COVERAGE AND THREE WEEKS VACATION."..IS THERE A CATCH?
NO, DUDE. NO CATCH. WISH ME LUCK...

THERE'S A CATCH.

RAT GETS A JOB AT A PARTY SUPPLY STORE
HEY, UH, ONE LAST THING... AS PART OF THE JOB, WE GIVE YOU A COMPANY CAR.
6/19

SWEET, PHIL...WHY DIDN'T YOU TELL ME EARLIER? THAT SAVES ME FROM HAVING TO TAKE THE STUPID BUS TO WORK.
YEAH...I SHOULD'VE MENTIONED IT..I'LL HAVE IT BROUGHT OVER AND SEE HOW YOU LIKE IT....

I'M NOT PLEASED, PHIL.

WHAT ARE YOU GUYS DOING?
We bury mines. If you walk in yard, you essplode.

DO YOU KNOW WHERE THEY'RE BURIED?
Ah. Gud idea. Larry, go in house. Make map.

BOOM
No go dat way.
6/20

GOOD EVENING, ESTEEMED CITIZENS...I AM YOUR BELOVED MAYOR...YOU CAN TELL THAT I'M BELOVED BY THE SMILING PEOPLE WHO HAVE CHOSEN TO SPONTANEOUSLY GATHER BEHIND ME.

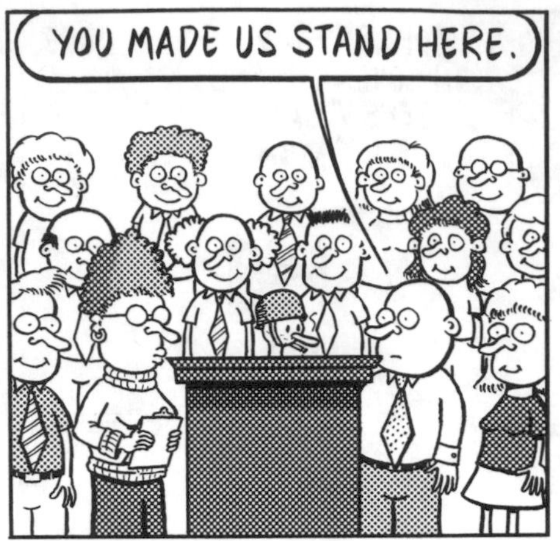
6/21
YOU MADE US STAND HERE.

SHOOT HIM.

LOOKS LIKE OUR MAYOR GOT CAUGHT SPYING ON PEOPLE... RATHER THAN FACE IMPEACHMENT, HE'S CHOSEN TO RESIGN.

6/22
WELL, AT LEAST NOW HE'LL HAVE TO DEPART THE OFFICE IN SHAME WITH HIS HEAD HUNG LOW...I CAN'T WAIT TO SEE THE LOOK OF DEFEAT ON HIS FACE....

HELLO, PIG.
FARINA, MY GERMOPHOBIC SISTER WHO LIVES IN A BUBBLE AND ONCE DATED RAT!...WHAT BRINGS YOU HERE?

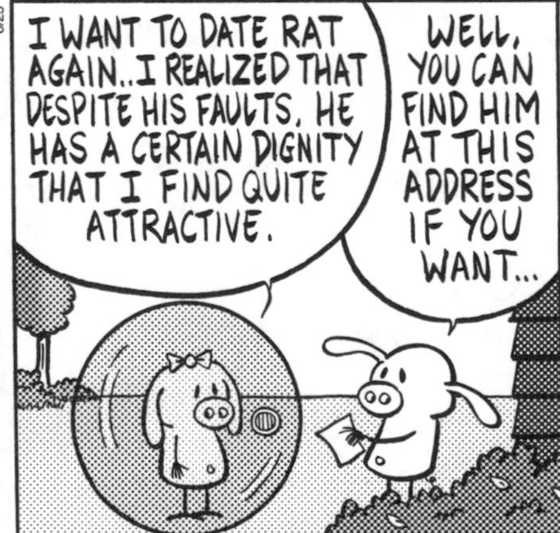
6/23
I WANT TO DATE RAT AGAIN..I REALIZED THAT DESPITE HIS FAULTS, HE HAS A CERTAIN DIGNITY THAT I FIND QUITE ATTRACTIVE.
WELL, YOU CAN FIND HIM AT THIS ADDRESS IF YOU WANT...

SO I SAW ON THE 'ANIMAL CHANNEL' THAT EVERY GROUP OF CROCS HAS A DOMINANT MALE, THE FIERCEST KILLER IN THE BUNCH...DO YOU GUYS HAVE ONE?

HAHAHAHA... Duuuh...Here, is me. Me has no conshuss. Me no put up wid nutting. Me a regular Deniss Meniss to Society.

You ?..Oh peese...Everyone know is me...You juss eediot.

You shut mouf.

You shut mouf.

6/24

Me telling.
MAMAAAAAAA Bob say 'Shut mouf.'
OHHH LORD.

I'M STARTING A TABLOID...I'M GONNA SPREAD LIES ABOUT EVERYONE I KNOW.
THAT BETTER NOT INCLUDE ME.

CLICK

NATIONAL ENQUIRAT
SHOCKING PHOTOS
ZEBRA EXPLODES IN NIGHT OF RAGE
FOUR STABBED WITH GREASY SPORK
SUBSTANCE ABUSE SUSPECTED!
BOYHOOD TOWN FEELS "GREAT SHAME"
"I thought I knew him," says former associate

MONEY MONEY MONEY MONEY MONEY MONEY

OKAY, RAT..EITHER YOU KNOCK OFF WHAT YOU'RE DOING WITH THAT TABLOID OF YOURS OR YOU'RE GONNA START LOSING YOUR FRIENDS.
LOSE MY FRIENDS? BUT THAT WOULD KILL ME.

YEAH, WELL YOU BETTER THINK ABOUT IT THEN, 'CAUSE I WILL WALK RIGHT OUT OF YOUR LIFE.
YOU? I THOUGHT YOU WERE TALKING ABOUT ABE, ULYSSES AND BENJAMIN.

FORGET IT.
Shhhhhh... HE'S LEAVING NOW, LITTLE BUDDIES.

Okay, zeeba neighba..Prepare to die. We have Mexican wrestler on our side.
HAHA Yeah.. Me crush you.
MEXICAN WRESTLERS SPEAK SPANISH.

Burrito. Burrito. Burrito.

Nice.

THWACK

Nachos. Nachos. Nachos.

OHHH, DEAR... I CAN'T FIND MY MONEY.
IT'S DOWN HERE ON THE FLOOR, MA'AM..YOU MUST HAVE DROPPED IT.

OHHHH, THANK YOU, SONNY...YOU'RE A SWEET DEAR.
KISS

CLICK

NATIONAL ENQUIRAT
EXPLICIT PHOTOS
PIG SNAGGED IN LURID TRYST
"Sick sick sick" says cop
MOTHER DISOWNS DEGENERATE SON
SCORNED EX LEFT TO PICK UP PIECES
PAYS CASH FOR AFFECTION
EXPLICIT PHOTOS

YOU'RE REALLY HURTING PEOPLE WITH THIS TABLOID YOU'RE PRINTING, RAT.
YES, BUT I'M GETTING RICH.

BUT IT'S NOT RIGHT.
DOING RIGHT IS TO MAKING MONEY WHAT DEFLATING THE TIRES IS TO RIDING A BICYCLE.

YOU MAY NOT BE ACHIEVING SAINTHOOD.
BUT I'LL BE RIDING A FAST BIKE.

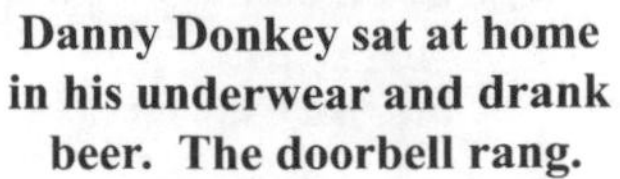

Danny Donkey sat at home in his underwear and drank beer. The doorbell rang.

"Help save the planet," said the people at his door. "Huh?" said Danny Donkey.

"Sign a petition. Attend a rally. Display a bumper sticker."

"I would like to sit at home in my underwear and drink beer," said Danny Donkey.

"But what does that accomplish?" asked the people.

"The beer that I am holding will go from full to empty," said Danny Donkey, "and I will be happy."

And at that, the people wept, for they realized the genius that was Danny Donkey.

OHHHHH, MAN... MY HEAD IS JUST KILLING ME... YOU GOT ANY ASPIRIN?
YEAH... I THINK I GOT A COUPLE IN MY POCKET.

7/2
CLICK
NATIONAL ENQUIRAT
REVOLTING PHOTOS
DRUG-ADDLED GOAT BUSTED IN MASSIVE NARCOTICS STING
From Altar Boy to Altered Boy: One Goat's Descent Into Sin p. 29

Okay, zeeba neighba... We tired of you games. We buy Spaneesh phrase book. Give wrestler fierce Spaneesh name...'Donde Está El Queso De Mi Padre'!

7/3
"WHERE IS MY FATHER'S CHEESE"?

Dat not dat fierce.

Hold me. Make my probblims go away.

7/4
YOU DUMB PIG... PROBLEMS DON'T GO AWAY JUST BECAUSE SOMEONE HOLDS YOU... PROBLEMS NEVER GO AWAY.
Hold me. Make my probblims go away.

Hold me
anyways.

Hola, Señor Zeebo... Me is dangerouso. Me can snappo necko. You geev uppo.
YOU KNOW... THAT WRESTLING IS AN ACT, LIKE A MAGIC SHOW OR A PLAY... THEY DON'T ACTUALLY HURT EACH OTHER.
Ack

SNAP

Ta-daaaaa.

HEY, BEETLE BAILEY.. HOW GOES IT?
HEY, PIG.. HANG ON A SEC...I GOTTA SAY A COUPLE THINGS TO ZERO... HE'S BEING SENT HOME FOR A WHILE.
IT'S OKAY. I GOTTA BE TAKING OFF ANYHOW.

OKAY.. BUT LISTEN... YOU TAKE CARE OF YOURSELF.
YOU TOO.
PAT PAT
PAT PAT

CLICK
NATIONAL ENQUIRAT
REVEALING PHOTOS!
DON'T ASK DON'T TELL?
SARGE: "I'M NOT PLEASED"

WHOA!...WHERE ARE YOU GOING, RAT?

I'M RUNNING AWAY FROM LIFE AND ALL MY PROBLEMS.

WOOHOOHOOOOOOOOO

I DIDN'T KNOW IT WAS THAT EASY.

WHAT ARE YOU DOING, L'IL GUARD DUCK?
I AM WAITING FOR MY GIRLFRIEND MAURA TO RETURN. SHE'S THE DUCK WHO FLEW SOUTH LAST WINTER AND BROKE MY HEART, SIR.

WHY DON'T YOU GO AND TRY TO FIND HER?
BECAUSE I CANNOT FLY, SIR. I HAVE TOLD YOU THAT, SIR. I AM A BROKEN DUCK, SIR.

THEN I WILL *HELP* YOU FLY, LITTLE GUARD DUCK. AND YOU WILL FIND HER. AND YOU WILL HAVE TRUE LOVE!

AND YOUR DAYS OF HAVING A BROKEN HEART WILL BE FOREVER GONE!!!

TOSS
THUD

I'M A BIRD, NOT A JAVELIN, SIR.
HOW 'BOUT WE JUST HAVE SOME CHOCOLATE AND A GOOD CRY?

I DON'T UNDERSTAND IT. I'M MAKING ALL THIS MONEY PUBLISHING A TABLOID, BUT I'M STILL NOT HAPPY.

AH...AND WHAT LESSON DOES THAT TEACH YOU?

THAT I MUST NOT BE MAKING ENOUGH MONEY.

WRONG LESSON.
WELL, I'M OFF TO RUIN SOME MORE LIVES.
7/9

HEY THERE, RAT... DID YOU SEE MY NEW STEREO?
WHAT KIND IS IT?

Heeeeey, LITTLE COFFEE MUG... DOING ANYTHING FRIDAY?... THE WIFE'S OUT OF TOWN AND—
YOUR WIFE'S RIGHT HERE, CLARENCE!
7/10

HIGH INFIDELITY.

YOU KNOW, I KNOW YOUR WIFE DOES YOUR HUNTING FOR YOU, BUT COULD YOU HUNT IF YOU HAD TO?
7/11

Oh yeah... But that's not a big deal... All it takes is a willingness to kill and a minimum level of competence.

Me hate you lots.

YOU KNOW, I HOPE YOUR MAKING MONEY FROM THIS TABLOID DOESN'T TURN YOU INTO ONE OF THOSE RICH JERKS WHO'S GOTTA HIRE PEOPLE TO DO EVERYTHING FOR THEM.

NO, I MAY BUY CARS AND STUFF BUT HIRING PEOPLE JUST ISN'T MY... AHHHHHHCHOOOOO

WIPE MY NOSE, PIG.
REGULAR OR EXTRA SOFT?
7/12

HELLO, STEPHAN PASTIS, CREATOR OF 'PEARLS.'
YOU MIND MOVING THE DRINK? WATER CAN RUIN MY DRAWINGS.
BEER
7/13

IT'S NOT WATER. IT'S BEER.
SAME THING.
BEER

POURRRRRR
BEER

I REALLY SHOULD TAKE YOUR WORD FOR IT.

...AND THEN WHEN HE GOT SHOT LIKE THAT, I COULDN'T BELIEVE IT.... I STILL CAN'T GET OVER IT...
WHAT ARE YOU GUYS TALKING ABOUT?

THAT 'SOPRANOS' ENDING...HOW THE GUY IN THE 'MEMBERS ONLY' JACKET SHOT TONY.
WHAT ARE YOU TALKING ABOUT? MY SCREEN JUST WENT BLACK.

BLACK?... WOW... SOUNDS LIKE A PROBLEM WITH YOUR CABLE... YOU SHOULD CALL SOMEONE...
AAAAAAA

7/14
WE'LL PAY FOR THIS.
YOU ONLY LIVE ONCE.
CLINK

I HAVE A CONFESSION TO MAKE.

WHAT IS IT?
EVERY TIME YOU LEAVE THE HOUSE, I GO INTO YOUR PUZZLE CABINET AND STEAL A PUZZLE PIECE.
7/15

YOU WHAT?
I'M A PUZZLE PILFERER.. THERE ARE MILLIONS OF US.

SO EVERY TIME I MAKE A PUZ-ZLE AND THERE'S ONE PIECE MISSING.....
....IT'S NO COINCIDENCE. BUT LUCKY FOR YOU, I'VE DECIDED TO GIVE 'EM BACK.

FOOOOSH....

.... STILL FRIENDS?

YOU BET... I'M JUST HAPPY YOU DECIDED TO GIVE 'EM BACK.

SNATCH

PEOPLE **CAN** CHANGE.

HEY GOAT... WHAT ARE YOU DOING?
I'M ON A DATE. DO YOU MIND?

WHOA...WELL, AT LEAST I WON'T HAVE TO WORRY ABOUT BEING CAST INTO THE FLAMES OF HELL WHEN I DIE.
WHY DO YOU SAY THAT?

BECAUSE HELL HATH FROZEN OVER.
PLEASE LEAVE.

GOAT GOES ON A DATE.
..SO...UH...WE'VE HAD A LOT OF RAIN LATELY, HUH?
YEAH.

YOU HAVE NICE HAIR.
THANKS.

DID YOU KNOW THAT THE WORD 'ZIP' IN 'ZIP CODE' STANDS FOR 'ZONING IMPROVEMENT PLAN'?

IT'S REALLY A WONDER YOU DON'T GET MORE DATES.

WELL, I GUESS THIS IS GOODNIGHT.
I GUESS IT IS.

ERRRT ERRRT ERRRRT AWKWARD MOMENT ALERT!!!

ADMITTEDLY, THE MEGAPHONE WAS OVERKILL.

Zeeba neighba? Dat you?
WHAT THE? WHAT HAVE YOU DONE TO MY HOUSE??

7/19
We go Home Depot. Spend savings on breek and ceement. Cover you doors and weendows. Now you trapped. Now we keel you.
AND HOW ARE YOU GONNA GET *IN*?

Dis not proudest moment.

WHY DOES THE ANONYMITY OF THE INTERNET BRING OUT THE WORST IN PEOPLE?
HOW DO YOU MEAN?

7/20
WELL, I KEEP THIS BLOG AND EVERY DAY THIS IDIOT POSTS COMMENTS RIPPING INTO MY WRITING... SO TODAY I POSTED THIS BASIC, FUNDAMENTAL QUESTION TO HIM: "WHY BOTHER READING SOMETHING YOU HATE?"

Oh. So profound.

LOOKS LIKE THE LIONS TOOK MY COUSIN LOU FROM THE BACK OF THE HERD LAST WEEK AND ATE HIM.
WHY DO ZEBRAS HANG OUT IN HERDS IF ALL THEY DO WHEN LIONS ATTACK IS STAND AROUND AND STARE AT THE GUY BEING DRAGGED OFF?

OHHH... WE DO A LOT MORE THAN THAT.
WHAT DO YOU DO?
7/21

WE WAVE GOODBYE.

It was Betty's tenth wedding anniversary. And she wanted to do something special.

So she and George rented a place by the sea.

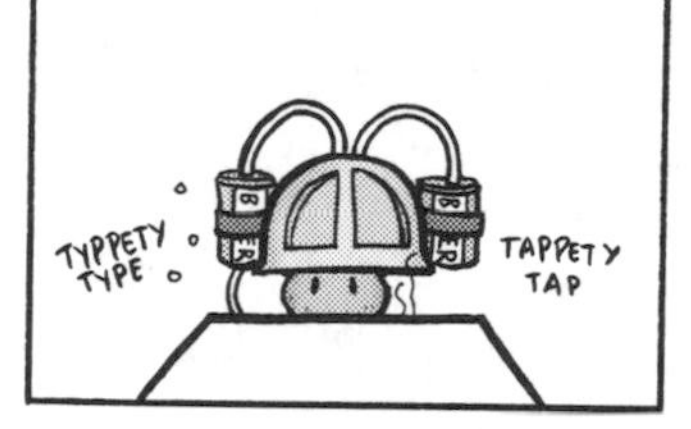

They sat on the deck. They listened to the ocean. They took long walks on the beach.

And when it was over, she turned to George and looked into his eyes. "We should go now, George," she said...

"... before Bob starts wondering where I am on our anniversary."

"Arf arf," replied George, wagging his tail.

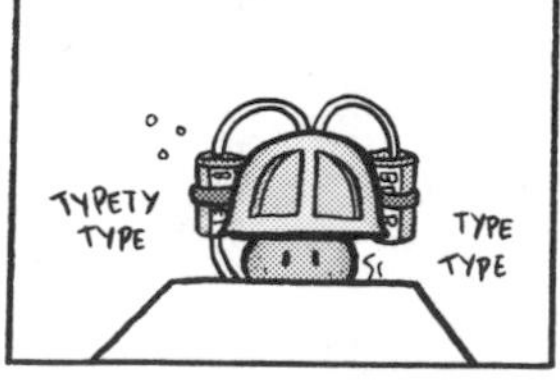

YOU NEED TO STOP WRITING ROMANCE NOVELS.

"Sometimes I think you love that dog more than me," said Bob. "Oh shut up," said Betty.

WHO'S THAT STANDING BEHIND US?
THAT'S CONNIE, THE JUDGMENTAL COW. SHE WATCHES YOU FROM A DISTANCE AND JUDGES EVERYTHING YOU DO.

GET USED TO IT, FATTY.

7/23
I DON'T THINK I LIKE HER.

WHAT ARE YOU DRAWING?
A CUTE LITTLE HOUSE...WHAT DO YOU THINK?

BOOOOOOOOOO

7/24
I'M GETTING TIRED OF CONNIE THE JUDGMENTAL COW.

"And so, da witch invited Hansel and Gretel into her candy-covered house. 'I will eat dem both,' she muttered.

But juss as she grabbed for da keeds, dey shoved her into da oven and ran away."

7/25
SNIFFLE
SNIFFLE
WHIMPER
SNIFFLE

IT'S NOT SUPPOSED TO BE A TRAGEDY, DAD.
But me HATE doze killer keeds.

WHAT ARE YOU WRITING?
A SHORT STORY. I THINK IF I WORK REALLY HARD, I CAN GET IT PUBLISHED.

AND MONKEYS WILL FLY OUT OF MY BUM.

CURSE THAT CONNIE THE JUDGMENTAL COW.

HAVE YOU SEEN MY NEW iPHONE?
IS THAT THE ONE THAT LETS YOU SURF THE INTERNET AND LISTEN TO MUSIC?

YES, AND IF YOU PRESS THIS BUTTON, IT DOES YOUR LAUNDRY AND BRINGS YOU A BEER.

NOW THAT'S A PHONE.

WHO'S THAT?
WILHELM, THE AQUATIC LAMB.

SINCE WHEN DO LAMBS LIVE IN THE OCEAN?
SINCE WILHELM CONVINCED HIS ENTIRE FLOCK TO MOVE THERE AS A WAY TO ESCAPE THE WOLVES.

WHERE'S HIS FLOCK?
THE SHARKS ATE THEM.

POOR LEADERSHIP SKILLS.

Hullooooo zeeba neighba... How you like try "Box O' Funn"?
7/29
BOX O' Funn

WHY WOULD I STEP INTO A BOX OF CROCODILES?
Is Box O' Funn! No can you see?
BOX O' Funn

YEAH, I SEE... BUT WHY WOULD I BELIEVE IT?
Becuss it print-ed right dere in *words*. Dat make it true.
BOX O' Funn

OKAY THEN....

BOX O' Morons

BOX O' Morons

Me want get out now.
BOX O' Morons

Alright now.... Slowly... Slowly....
WHAT ARE YOU GUYS DOING?
DEAD ZEBRA

The wives left us. We lost our household's primary prey-earners.
SO WHAT'S THAT?
7/30

Court-ordered support.
Want some?
NO THANKS.

I DON'T UNDERSTAND...YOU GUYS GET DIVORCED AND YOUR WIVES OWE YOU ALL THIS SUPPORT...BUT YOU'RE PERFECTLY CAPABLE OF GOING OUT AND HUNTING YOURSELVES.
DEAD ZEBRA
7/31

We had a good lawyer.
DEAD ZEBRA

I TRY NOT TO BRAG.

WHAT ARE YOU DOING BEING A LAWYER?...I THOUGHT YOU WERE MAKING PLENTY OF CASH PUBLISHING A TABLOID.
I WAS. BUT I GOT BORED.

SO I ASKED MYSELF, WHAT JOB ALLOWS ME TO MAKE A GOOD LIVING WHILE HELPING OTHERS AND FURTHERING THE CAUSE OF JUSTICE?
8/1

SNICKER
SNICKER
SNICKER

I ALWAYS LAUGH WHEN I SAY THAT.

WHAT'S WITH THE OUTFIT, JUNIOR?
I'VE DECIDED THAT CROCS SHOULD REALLY START WEARING CLOTHES...IT'S JUST NOT CIVILIZED TO WALK AROUND WITHOUT PANTS.
WHAT'S YOUR DAD THINK?

WOOHOOO

HE'S RESISTING.

I'VE DECIDED TO FIND ALL MY ENEMIES AND TELL THEM I FORGIVE THEM.

GOOD FOR YOU, RAT...WHY'D YOU DECIDE TO DO THAT?

TO GIVE MY VENGEANCE THE ELEMENT OF SURPRISE.

WHAT ARE YOU READING?
THE CLASSIFIEDS. I'M LOOKING FOR A USED CAR. THIS CHEVY VEGA LOOKS CHEAP.

OH, THOSE CARS ARE THE BEST....YOU CAN DO WHATEVER YOU WANT IN THEM AND NOT WORRY ABOUT A THING.
WHY DO YOU SAY THAT?

WHAT HAPPENS IN VEGAS STAYS IN VEGAS.

MAYBE I GOT THAT WRONG.

I CAN'T BELIEVE IT... ALL THIS TIME HAS PASSED AND I STILL CAN'T GET OVER THE 'SOPRANOS' ENDING... HOW THE SCREEN JUST WENT BLACK...
8/5

OH, WOW... YOU SHOULD HAVE SAID SOMETHING... I'M PERSONAL FRIENDS WITH THE WRITER, DAVID CHASE... MATTER OF FACT, HE'S HERE NOW...

OH MY GOD! DAVID CHASE! I CAN'T BELIEVE IT! YOU'VE GOT TO TELL ME WHAT HAPPENS! PLEASE PLEASE PLEASE PLEASE PLEASE!

HAHAHA... NO PROBLEM... WELL, AFTER THE FELLOW IN THE 'MEMBERS ONLY' JACKET MAKES THAT TURN TOWARD THE RESTROOM, HE —

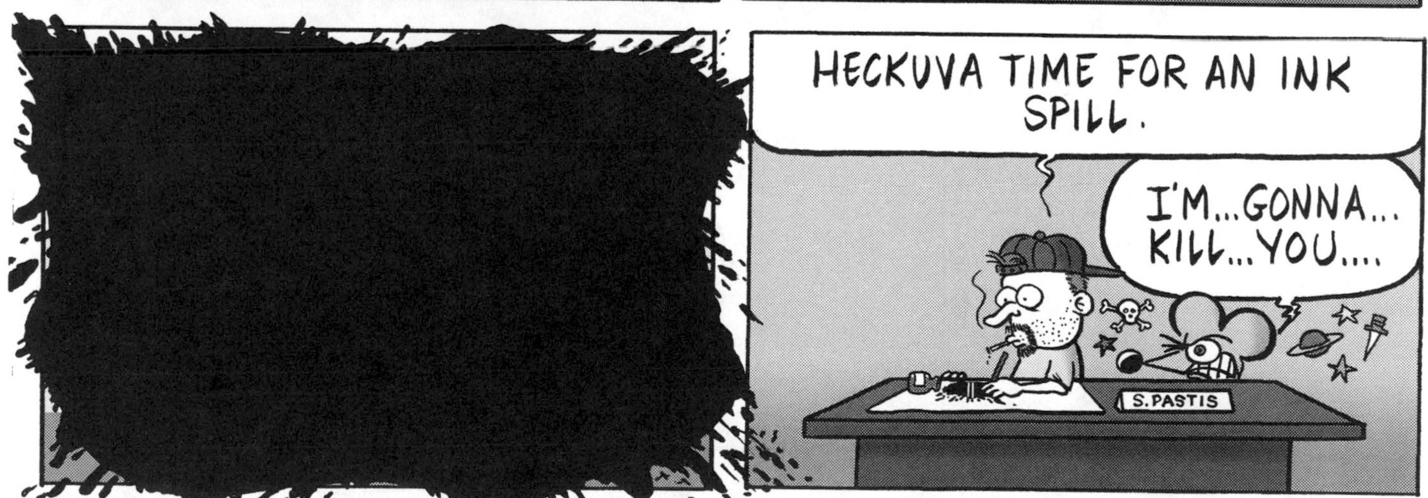
HECKUVA TIME FOR AN INK SPILL.
I'M... GONNA... KILL... YOU....
S. PASTIS

THE CROCODILE'S INNATE ABILITY TO REMAIN MOTIONLESS FOR HOURS IS THE KEY TO HIS DEADLY HUNTING PROWESS.

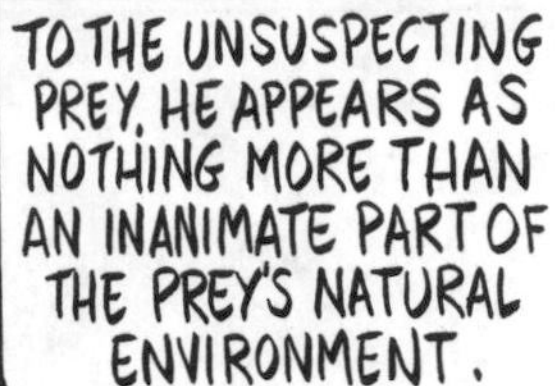
TO THE UNSUSPECTING PREY, HE APPEARS AS NOTHING MORE THAN AN INANIMATE PART OF THE PREY'S NATURAL ENVIRONMENT.

8/6

RAT, THIS IS SAM. HE'S LOOKING FOR A JOB. SAM IS ONE OF THE MOST UNIQUE AND EXOTIC BIRDS IN ALL OF NORTH AMERICA.

8/7
HE'S A PIGEON.

THAT'S ONE PADDED RÉSUMÉ.

WHAT ARE YOU DOING?
I'VE DECIDED TO BECOME A MIME... LOOK... I'M TRAPPED BEHIND A SOLID GLASS WALL.
8/8

KONK

I THINK I FOUND AN OPENING.

WHAT ARE YOU DOING, RAT?
BEHOLD! I AM EGO-MAN.

YOU'RE A SUPERHERO?
YES, BUT WITH A UNIQUE APPROACH TO HELPING OTHERS.

WHICH IS?
I DON'T.

OH, LORD.
EGO-MAN: DEFENDER OF ONLY HIMSELF.

THE ADVENTURES OF EGO-MAN, DEFENDER OF ONLY HIMSELF.
HELP! HELP! I'M BEING MUGGED!

EGO-MAN! SAVE ME! I'M BEING MUGGED!
YES, BUT HOW DOES THIS AFFECT *ME*?

I GUESS IT DOESN'T.

HOW COME EVERYONE SPENDS SO MUCH TIME FOCUSING ON HOW TO PROLONG THEIR LIVES AND SO LITTLE TIME ON HOW TO ACTUALLY *LIVE* THEIR LIVES?

IT'S SO STRANGE...IT'S LIKE OBSESSING ABOUT THE AMOUNT OF GAS LEFT IN YOUR TANK WHILE SPEEDING DOWN A HIGHWAY TO NOWHERE...WOULDN'T YOU LIKE TO KNOW WHY PEOPLE DO THAT?

WHAT I'D LIKE TO KNOW IS HOW I WOUND UP IN A DR. PHIL INFOMERCIAL.
NEVER MIND.

"DEFENDANT ZEBRA HAS WILLFULLY FAILED TO BE PLAINTIFFS' FOOD, IN BREACH OF NATURAL LAW... PLAINTIFFS SEEK DEFENDANT ZEBRA COOKED MEDIUM WELL OVER A BARBECUE PIT."

WHAT CHOICE DO YOU HAVE?

WELL, I HATE TO SAY IT, BUT I KNOW RAT JUST STARTED PRACTICING LAW... MAYBE HE CAN HELP OUT A FRIEND FOR FREE... AFTER ALL, MY LIFE IS ON THE LINE...

8/12

I HEAR ZEBRA GOT SUED BY THE CROCS.
YEAH. THEY SAY HE 'WILLFULLY FAILED' TO BE THEIR FOOD, AND THAT TWO-FACED FRIEND OF YOURS, RAT, IS REPRESENTING THEM.

8/13
THAT'S AWFUL. WHAT'S ZEBRA GONNA DO?
HIRE HIS OWN ATTORNEY. SOMEONE TOUGH... SOMEONE RUTHLESS.. SOMEONE WHO DOESN'T MESS AROUND...

YOU'VE COME TO THE RIGHT DUCK.
DUCK, ESQ. "Ethics Schmethics"

ZEBRA IS SUED BY THE CROCS
FIRST THING WE GOTTA DO IS CALL OPPOSING COUNSEL AND EXPLORE SETTLEMENT OPTIONS.
Beep Beep Boop

8/14
HELLO... COUNSELOR?... SETTLE OR I FIREBOMB YOUR OFFICE.

SETTLE OR I BEAT YOU SILLY.

THAT DIDN'T GO WELL.

IS IT REALLY TRUE YOU'RE SUING THE ZEBRA, DAD?
Oh, yes, son. See, in Amereeca, when you want someteeng, you juss sue.
Beer

8/15
BUT THAT SEEMS UNFAIR... ZEBRA'S DONE NOTHING WRONG... THAT WOULD BE LIKE ME SUING MY SCHOOL DISTRICT JUST TO GET BETTER GRADES.
Ohh, son... You no get it... Legal system is like Lotto, only wid better odds and no ping pong balls!

ABOUT THAT SCHOOL DISTRICT...
NO THANKS.
Scratch and ween, son! Scratch and ween!
Beer

ZEBRA IS SUED BY THE CROCS
SO WHAT'S YOUR STRATEGY FOR DEFEND-ING ME?
I'LL MAKE A MOTION TO COMPEL THE CROCS' DEPOSITIONS.. THAT'S WHERE I ASK 'EM STUFF UNDER OATH.

WHAT IF THEY REFUSE TO ANSWER?

I MAKE PRETTY COMPELLING MOTIONS.

ZEBRA IS SUED BY THE CROCS
I DON'T GET IT, COUNSELOR... YOUR CLIENTS ARE SUING THE ZEBRA FOR 'FAILURE TO BE FOOD.'..BUT WHY CAN'T THEY JUST HUNT HIM DOWN LIKE OTHER PREDATORS DO?

BECAUSE, YOUR HONOR, MY CLIENTS ARE IDIOTS... MORONS, DOOFUSES, DUNDERHEADS, FOOLS, BUFFOONS, BONEHEADS, HALFWITS, NUMSKULLS, SIMPLETONS, STOOGES, FATHEADS, CHUMPS, CLOWNS, CRETINS...

Dat problee enough.

ZEBRA IS SUED BY THE CROCS: THE DEPOSITION.
NOW THAT THE PLAINTIFF HAS BEEN SWORN IN, I'D LIKE TO BEGIN ASK-ING MY QUESTIONS... SIR, PLEASE STATE YOUR NAME.

I OBJECT. I OBJECT TO YOU. I OBJECT TO YOUR FACE. AND YOUR MAMA'S FAT.

THIS COULD GET CONTENTIOUS.

I DON'T UNDERSTAND THESE SOAP OPERA STRIPS. ALL THEY DO IS EXTEND OUT NORMAL CONVERSATIONS, ITALICIZE EVERY THIRD WORD, SHOW A BUNCH OF CLOSE-UPS, AND END WITH A SHOT OF SOME IDIOT STARING AT A PHONE.
COMICS

...YOU MEAN...?

YES!...

I THINK...

WE COULD DO THAT!
!

...BUT WHAT ABOUT...

THE NARRATOR ?!
YES!
GOT IT... PARTNER!

AND DON'T FORGET...

WHAT ?!?

...THE PHONE!
WILL IT... RING?!
TO BE CONTINUED...

ZEBRA IS SUED BY THE CROCS

COUNSEL, I'VE CALLED YOU IN HERE BECAUSE I'VE GOT WORD OF SOME UNPROFESSIONAL BEHAVIOR DURING PRE-TRIAL PROCEEDINGS.

NOW AS I UNDERSTAND IT, MR. DUCK, YOU TRIED TO ASK QUESTIONS OF MR. RAT'S CLIENTS AND MR. RAT DID WHAT?
HE BEGAN MAKING 'YOUR MAMA' JOKES.

UNBELIEVABLE. AND HOW DID YOU RESPOND?
I PUSHED HIS PARALEGAL OUT A SIXTH STORY WINDOW.

OHHHHH LORD.
I SAID I WAS SORRY, YOUR HONOR.
TOO BAD SHE DIDN'T BOUNCE OFF YOUR MAMA.

Hey, Meester Attorney Man. Me get big bill from you. Me not like.
TOO BAD, PAL... I ACCOUNTED FOR EVERY HOUR I SPENT ON YOUR STUPID CASE.

"Shower: 2.0"?
YEP. I SPENT TWO HOURS THINKING ABOUT YOUR CASE IN THE SHOWER.

"Sleep: 7.0"?
I DREAMT ABOUT THE CASE... PERFECTLY LEGIT.

"Relieving Self: .5"?
WHERE I DO MY BEST THINKING. CONSIDER IT A BARGAIN.

WHO WAS ON THE PHONE?
MY SISTER FARINA... SHE WANTED ME TO TELL YOU SHE'S MET SOMEONE NEW AND IS MOVING WITH HIM TO FLORIDA.

WHY THAT LITTLE HOOCHIE! I'M SUPPOSED TO BE THE LOVE OF HER LIFE! THAT DOES IT... I'M GONNA TRAVEL TO FLORIDA AND GET THAT GUY!...

WHY ARE YOU WEARING AN ASTRONAUT HELMET AND DIAPERS?
IT SEEMED APPROPRIATE.

IS IT TRUE YOU'RE REALLY DRIVING ACROSS THE COUNTRY TO GET YOUR EX-GIRLFRIEND'S LOVER?
The Revenge O'Mobile

8/23
YES...I'VE GOT MY REVENGE-O'-MOBILE, MY HELMET AND MY MACE.
WELL, IF YOU'RE REALLY GONNA DO THAT, YOU OUGHT TO AT LEAST GO TO THE BATHROOM FIRST. THAT'S A LONG DRIVE.

DO YOU REALLY WANT ME TO DO THAT?
BACK IN THE CAR. BACK IN THE CAR.

LOOKS LIKE THE PLAINTIFFS ARE CAVING...THEY JUST FAXED ME A SETTLEMENT OFFER.
REALLY? WHAT ARE THEY OFFERING?

WELL, ORIGINALLY, THEY SOUGHT YOU COOKED MEDIUM WELL OVER A BARBECUE PIT.
I KNOW, I KNOW. IT WAS RIDICULOUS. WHAT NOW?

MEDIUM RARE.

8/24
WE SHOULD PROBABLY REJECT THIS.

ZEBRA IS SUED BY THE CROCS: THE TRIAL
COUNSEL FOR THE CROCS, WHY DON'T YOU GET STARTED WITH YOUR OPENING ARGUMENTS?

I'M SORRY, YOUR HONOR, I'M RAT'S CO-COUNSEL, PIG... HE ASKED ME TO ASK YOU FOR A... ..UH...CONTINUANCE?

WHAT FOR?

8/25
HE'S TRAVELING CROSS-COUNTRY IN DIAPERS TO KILL SOMEONE.

Me having doubts about counsel.

WHAT HAPPENED TO YOUR HOUSE?
We tear down. Swamp natural advannage. Ees all part of BEEG plan.

THAT'S MORONIC.
Ohhhhhh... Moroneec, huh? You not say dat when you ees keeled.

OH? AND HOW DO YOU PLAN TO DO THAT?
Unnerwater spear-gun. You fall een. We shoot. FOOM! You not know what happen.

WHERE'D YOU LEARN TO WORK ONE OF THOSE?
Learn? What dere learn? You juss pull—
FOOM!

8/26

Good ting he not know what happen.

SO THE CROCS NEXT DOOR TO ME HAVE FIGURED OUT THEY NEED LAND SPEED.
WHY IS THAT ?

8/27
BECAUSE CROCS IN THE WILD ARE CAPABLE OF TREMENDOUS BURSTS OF SPEED ON LAND, ALLOWING THEM TO SURPRISE THEIR PREY.
SO WHAT ARE THEY GONNA DO?

Zeeba good as dead.

RRRRRRRRRRR

RRRRRRR
You mine, @#$☆@.

FIVE MINUTES LATER.
8/28
I GOTTA GO.
RRRRRRR
Dang.

Putt Putt Putt Putt
The Revenge O'Mobile

The Revenge O'Mobile

RRRRRRRRRRR
Zeeba Assasin
The Revenge O'Mobile

8/29
WELL NOW HERE'S A SCENE YOU WOULDN'T FIND IN 'FOR BETTER OR FOR WORSE.'
The Revenge O'Mobile

SOMEWHERE NEAR SURPRISE, ARIZONA
PIG, IT'S ME, RAT. MY CAR BROKE DOWN. I NEED HELP, AND MAKE IT QUICK...MY CELL PHONE BATTERY IS DYING.
O'Mobile

OH MY GOODNESS..WHERE ARE YOU?
SURPRISE.
OH, I LOVE SURPRISES!
IT'S NOT A SURPRISE.

YOU SAID IT WAS A SURPRISE.
I DID NOT SAY IT WAS A SURPRISE.

THEN WHERE ARE YOU IF IT'S NOT A SURPRISE?
SURPRISE!
Beep beep beep
RAT, IS THAT YOUR CELL PHONE BATTERY WARNING?... RAT?...
RAT? RAT? RAT?

SOMEWHERE IN ARIZONA
SIR, PLEASE... HELP ME!..I'M DYING OF THIRST.
AREN'T YOU THAT L'IL RAT FROM THE FUNNIES THAT LIKES TO POKE FUN AT THE OLDER COMICS?

YES! YES! THAT'S ME! WHAT BRINGS YOU OUT HERE?

'FAMILY CIRCUS' CONVENTION, YOU LITTLE @☆@#!
BOOT
JEFFY IS GOD
DOLLY

THIS IS NOT GOOD.

RAT IS CAPTURED BY 'FAMILY CIRCUS' FANS
LISTEN, WHEN I POKE FUN OF 'FAMILY CIRCUS,' BIL KEANE LOVES IT...I SWEAR..HERE, GIVE ME YOUR CELL...I'LL PROVE IT!
THEL
ARFY
JEFFY

Beep Beep Boop Beep Boop Boop
BIL KEANE HERE.
Heeeeeeeey, BIL..IT'S ME, RAT, FROM 'PEARLS BEFORE SWINE'....

WHY YOU LITTLE @#☆@#
PERHAPS BIL'S HAVING A BAD MORNING.
ARFY

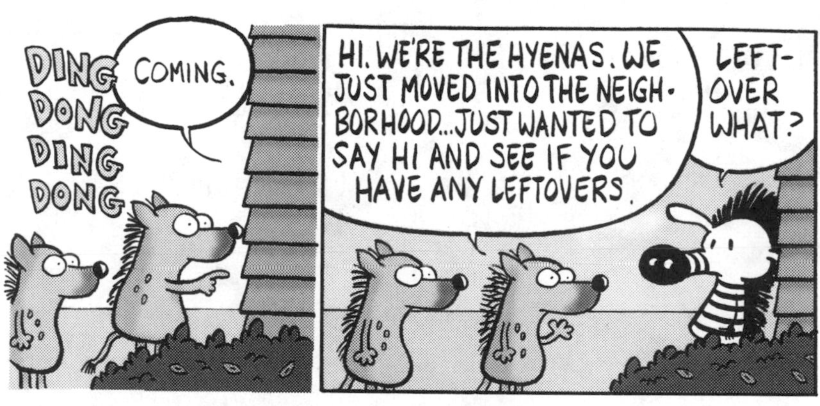
DING DONG DING DONG
COMING.
HI. WE'RE THE HYENAS. WE JUST MOVED INTO THE NEIGH-BORHOOD...JUST WANTED TO SAY HI AND SEE IF YOU HAVE ANY LEFTOVERS.
LEFT-OVER WHAT?

DEAD GUYS. WE'RE NOT PICKY.
WHAT, YOU THINK I'M GONNA LET YOU EAT ONE OF MY RELATIVES?

JUST A DEAD ONE. MAYBE AN UNCLE OR SOMETHING.

YOU LISTEN TO ME...IF ONE OF MY RELATIVES DIES, I TAKE THEM TO A FUNERAL HOME...FOR A *PROPER* BURIAL...ONE FILLED WITH RESPECT AND LOVE AND DIGNITY!
SLAM!

DING DONG
HY AND HY FUNERAL HOME

C'MON, BIL... TELL YOUR CRAZY FANS YOU LOVE IT WHEN WE PARODY YOUR COMIC.
TELL ME..WHICH PART DID I LOVE?
WAS IT WHEN YOU HAD THE KIDS HUGGING THEIR "DEAD GRANDPA"?

"We love you, dead Grandpa."

WAS IT WHEN JEFFY WAS A FELON?

"And remember...No telling Mommy I shot my probation officer."

OR WAS IT WHEN YOU HAD OSAMA BIN LADEN LIVING WITH THEM?

"I'm sorry, Osama, but at the end of grace, we say, 'Amen,' not 'Death to America.'"

YOU'RE GONNA LET ME GET KILLED, AREN'T YOU, BIL?
OH, NOT ME.

NOT ME

RAT! YOU ESCAPED FROM THE 'FAMILY CIRCUS' FANS!..HOW'D YOU DO IT?
I HAD TO PROMISE BIL KEANE WE'D NEVER WANDER INTO THE 'FAMILY CIRCUS' AGAIN. OH, AND WE HAVE TO LET HIS CHARACTERS WANDER INTO *OUR* STRIP NOW AND THEN.

BUT WE'RE SO DARK, AND THEY'RE SO SWEET.
OH, PLEASE. COMIC STRIP HUMOR IS COMIC STRIP HUMOR.

"It's raining! It's raining! That means God is crying."

I'VE MADE A TERRIBLE MISTAKE.

THE 'FAMILY CIRCUS' INVADES 'PEARLS BEFORE SWINE'
ALRIGHT, JEFFY...IF YOU'RE GONNA STAY, YOU'RE GONNA HAVE TO MAKE SOME CHANGES.

"Like what?"

LIKE STOP TALKING UNDER THE PANELS!...IT'S HARD TO SEE.

"That's your problem."

HEY! HEY! THAT'S *MY* SPACE.

"Alright, smart@##, what are you gonna do now?"

HI, PIGITA. SORRY I'M LATE.
YOU BETTER BE. IT'S OUR SEVENTH ANNIVERSARY... AND WHAT'S THAT?

A 'SLINKY'...YOU KNOW, "IT'S SLINKY, IT'S SLINKY, FOR FUN IT'S A WONDERFUL TOY."
WHY WOULD YOU BRING A G#☆#G☆! SLINKY TO AN EVENT AS IMPORTANT AS OUR ANNIVERSARY DINNER?

I THOUGHT WE WERE EXCHANGING GIFTS.

I GUESS WE'RE NOT EXCHANGING GIFTS.

AFTER MUCH STUDY, I HAVE DETERMINED THE CAUSE OF GLOBAL WARMING.

AND WHAT IS THAT?
IDIOTS THE WORLD OVER SPOUTING THEIR WORTHLESS OPINIONS...THE EXCESSIVE HOT AIR IS KILLING US.

BEFORE YOU RETORT, CONSIDER THE ENVIRONMENTAL CONSEQUENCES.

WHO'S YOUR FRIEND?
TIMMY THE ZOMBIE. I WAS LISTENING TO MY 'IPOD' IN THE GRAVEYARD AND HE FOLLOWED ME HOME.

WHY'D YOU BRING HIM HERE?
I DUNNO. I FIGURED IT'S BEEN A LONG TIME SINCE HE HAD A NICE MEAL, SO I THOUGHT I'D TREAT HIM TO SOME FRIED CHEESE STICKS.

FRIED CHEESE STICKS? THOSE THINGS'LL GIVE YOU A CORONARY.

HE'S NOT TOO CONCERNED ABOUT CORONARIES.

HEY, RAT... WHAT'S JEFFY FROM THE 'FAMILY CIRCUS' DOING HERE?
IT'S PART OF A DEAL. OUR CHARACTERS ARE ALWAYS WANDERING INTO THE 'FAMILY CIRCUS,' SO WE'RE LETTING THEIR CHARACTERS HANG OUT HERE.

THAT'S GREAT...THE 'FAMILY CIRCUS' IS SO SWEET.. WHAT DID YOU DO TODAY, LITTLE JEFFY?

"I hugged my mommy. I played with Barfy. I mispronuncicated some of my words. Then I came here to this restaurant."

WOW! YOU WERE A BUSY BOY, JEFFY! HEY, I KNOW! LET'S LOOK BACK AND SEE THAT DOTTED TRAIL OF EVERYTHING YOU DID!

"Well, I don't know if that's really necessary....I mean, I --"

GANG INITIATION

STEAL CAR
ROB LIQUOR STORE

GET SOME TATS

"So I'm battling a few demons."

RAT, ESQUIRE... RAT SPEAKING.
Hullo, Rat... Is me, croc. We want dismiss lawsoot against zeeba.
BEER
BEER

DISMISS IT? YOU'RE INSANE. YOU THINK YOU'RE GONNA CATCH THAT ZEBRA ON YOUR OWN?
Yes. And me will have da Jiffy dessert, too.
BEER
BEER

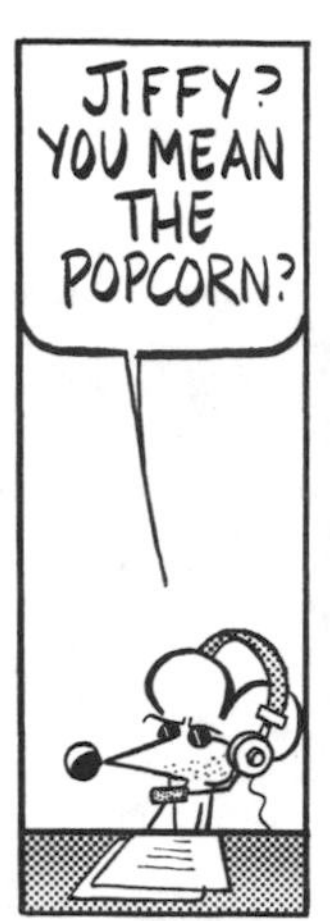

JIFFY? YOU MEAN THE POPCORN?

"It's 'Jeffy,' not 'Jiffy.'"

RAT! RAT! ZEBRA GOT CAUGHT BY THE CROCS!
HOW'D THAT HAPPEN?

LITTLE JEFFY THOUGHT THE CROCS' SWAMP WAS A SWIMMING POOL AND DOVE IN! ZEBRA TRIED TO SAVE HIM AND THE CROCS CAUGHT THEM *BOTH!*
SO THAT'S WHY THE CROCS MADE ME DISMISS THEIR SUIT! I'LL HAVE TO DO SOMETHING FAST.

YES, BUT WHAT?
SEND THEM MY FINAL BILL.

I MEANT ABOUT ZEBRA.
DON'T TELL ME ***HE*** OWES ME MONEY.

ZEBRA, BEFORE WE DIE, I'D LIKE TO ASK YOU JUST ONE QUESTION... WHY'D YOU RISK YOUR LIFE TO SAVE ME?

BECAUSE, JEFFY, I LIKE YOU... YOU REPRESENT INNOCENCE... A TIME IN AMERICA WHEN THINGS WERE KINDER AND SIMPLER. A TIME WHEN PEOPLE CARED ABOUT ONE ANOTHER.

"Whatever."

YOU'RE KIND OF RUINING THE MOMENT, JEFFY.

"Zebra meat tastes guuuud."

Hullooo, zeeba neighba... Leesten... Me tink you was very lucky to escape us crocs dis week. We almost eat you alive.

YOU KNOW SOMETHING? I DON'T THINK YOU COULD HAVE ACTUALLY EATEN ME. I DON'T THINK YOUR CONSCIENCE WOULD'VE LET YOU.

Conshuss?...What is dis conshuss?

ME, MY SON. I AM YOUR CONSCIENCE. AND THE KILLING AND EATING OF OTHERS IS WRONG! YOU NEED TO *THINK* ABOUT YOUR ACTIONS!

TOSS

CHOMP
CHOMP
CHOMP
CHOMP

Me always tink better after leetle snack.

WELL, GUYS, I'M OFF.
WHERE TO?

FLYING HOME TO SEE MY FAMILY AND MY RELATIVES... I HAVEN'T BEEN HOME IN TWELVE YEARS.
HOW LONG YOU STAY-ING?

FORTY-FIVE MINUTES.

I DON'T LIKE TO PUSH MY LUCK.

GOAT FLIES HOME FOR THE FIRST TIME IN TWELVE YEARS
I'M SO NERVOUS...I HAVE SO MANY QUESTIONS... LIKE WHAT IF MY FAMILY'S CHANGED?...

...OR WHAT IF I'VE CHANGED? ..OR WHAT IF I HAVE NOTHING TO SAY TO THEM?...

...OR WHAT IF I SUFFOCATE BETWEEN TWO FAT GUYS IN COACH?
MOVE THE SNOUT, PAL. YOU'RE CROWDING MY ELBOW.

GOAT RETURNS HOME FOR THE FIRST TIME IN TWELVE YEARS
MOM!
SON!

THUD
BAG O' GUILT

YOU COULDN'T EVEN WAIT 'TIL I GOT IN THE FRONT DOOR?
NOPE.
BAG O' GUILT

GOAT RETURNS HOME TO SEE HIS FAMILY.
OH, SON... WE HAVE SO MUCH TO CATCH UP ON... BUT FIRST, EAT...EAT... YOU'RE MUCH TOO SKINNY...NOW HERE'S SOME—

SWEETHEART, YOU'VE BARELY TOUCHED YOUR FISH...IS THAT ALL YOU'RE GONNA EAT?

UM FUH, MAH.
FULL?.. ALREADY?

SO, SON, HOW'S YOUR WORK?
FINE, MA. I'VE BEEN IN THE COMIC STRIP FIVE YEARS NOW...DO YOU STILL READ IT?

YES, BUT I DON'T ALWAYS UNDERSTAND IT... AND WHY DO THEY CALL YOU 'GOAT'? YOUR NAME IS 'PARIS.'
I KNOW, MA. IT'S JUST A STAGE NAME.

WELL, IT'S A DUMB NAME IF YOU ASK ME.. AND WHY DO THEY GIVE ALL THE JOKES TO THAT RAT AND PIG? CAN'T YOU SAY FUNNY LINES?

HOW 'BOUT WE TALK ABOUT SOMETHING ELSE, MA?
SURE...

HOW COME YOU DON'T VISIT MORE OFTEN?

LIKE MOTHER TERESA, I HAVE FOUND A PURPOSE FOR MY LIFE.
THAT'S WONDERFUL! WHAT IS IT?

I AM GOING TO FIND EVERY IDIOT WHO'S EVER POSED FOR A PHOTO BY RESTING HIS CHIN ON THE BACK OF HIS HAND AND BEAT HIM WITH THIS CUCUMBER.

HEY, GUYS, LOOK! I JUST GOT MY PHOTO TAKEN, AND BOY, DO I LOOK THOUGHTFUL!
I'M SENSING A CUCUMBER MOMENT.
RUN, PIG, RUN...

Blah Blah
Blah Blah
HEY YOU.... PAY ATTENTION TO YOUR KID.

Blah
Blah
Blah
WHAT KIND OF DAD COMES ALL THE WAY TO THE PARK WITH HIS LITTLE GIRL AND THEN SPENDS HALF THE TIME ON HIS CELL PHONE?...WHAT'S THAT TEACHING YOUR KID?

SNATCH

FLING
SPLOOSH

THAT'S NOT MY KID.
9/23

LET'S GO, SWEETIE... I DON'T WANT YOU EXPOSED TO VIOLENCE...
WHAT'S THAT TEACHING KIDS?
SHAKE
SHAKE
SHAKE
SHAKE

GOAT RETURNS HOME FOR THE FIRST TIME IN TWELVE YEARS
I HOPE YOU DON'T MIND, SON, BUT I INVITED OVER SOME OF YOUR RELATIVES...THEY'RE IN THE BACKYARD...

YOU DID? WHY DIDN'T YOU TELL ME? WE HAVE SO MUCH TO TALK ABOUT.. SO MUCH CATCHING UP TO DO....

BAAAAAAH
SOMEBODY'S CHANGED, MA.
DON'T BE RUDE, SON... SAY HELLO.

SON, TALK TO YOUR UNCLE... HE HASN'T SEEN YOU IN TWELVE YEARS...
BUT I DON'T KNOW WHAT TO SAY....I DON'T UNDERSTAND HIM.

WHAT DO YOU MEAN YOU DON'T UNDERSTAND HIM?
HE'S...HE'S CHANGED... HE'S JUST A GOAT.. HE EATS GRASS. HE WALKS ON ALL FOURS.

OH, SON...HE DIDN'T CHANGE....YOU DID.
BAAAA

AND NOT FOR THE BETTER, SAYS YOUR PEEVED UNCLE TED.

WELL, GOODBYE, MOM.. I JUST WANT YOU TO KNOW I LOVE YOU... AND EVEN THOUGH A LOT OF WHAT YOU SAY IS FILLED WITH SUBTLE CRITICISM, I KNOW YOU DON'T MEAN IT.

I LOVE YOU TOO, SON...I LOVE YOU MORE THAN ANYTHING.

DID YOU SHOWER?

WHERE'S RAT TODAY?
HE GOT A 'JUSTICE OF THE PEACE' LICENSE...HE'S GONNA PERFORM WEDDINGS.
9/27

A CYNIC LIKE HIM?..THAT'S PROBABLY NOT A GOOD IDEA.
OHH, HE'LL BE FINE.

AND REMEMBER, 'GROOM' RHYMES WITH 'DOOM.'

RAT ACTS AS JUSTICE OF THE PEACE.
...AND NOW I'D LIKE TO INTRODUCE A DOVE, WHICH REPRESENTS THE PEACE AND HARMONY YOU TWO WILL EXPERIENCE TOGETHER.
9/28

AND BOBO THE ELEPHANT, WHO REPRESENTS THE PROBLEMS.

NO SUDDEN MOVES. BOBO'S JUMPY.

RAT, JUSTICE OF THE PEACE
BEFORE I JOIN THIS YOUNG COUPLE IN HOLY MATRIMONY, I'D LIKE TO SAY A FEW WORDS TO THE LOVELY BRIDE AND HER GROOM ABOUT THIS, THEIR SPECIAL DAY...
9/29

EACH OF YOU COULD HAVE DONE MUCH, MUCH BETTER.

YOUR MOTHERS MADE ME SAY THAT.

ANIMAL SHELTER
...THANKS AGAIN FOR ADOPTING THIS CAT... NOT EVERY PERSON THAT COMES IN HERE ASKS FOR THE CAT THAT SCRATCHES AND BITES THE MOST.
Oh... Ees no probbum. We nice guy.

♪

HEY... WHAT ARE YOU GUYS DOING WITH A—
KEEL ZEEBA
REEP TO SHRED

AWWWWW... CUTE L'IL GUY...
KEEL HEEM
TEAR OFF HEAD
Meow.

HOW 'BOUT I GET YOU SOME MILK...
Keel heem
End zeeba life
Mwowrrr

Cat must have secret plan.

LEMME MAKE SURE I UNDERSTAND...YOU MORONS ADOPTED A MEAN CAT TO KILL THE ZEBRA, BUT THE CAT TURNED OUT TO *LIKE* THE ZEBRA.
Peese shut mouf, woomun. You no unnerstan nutting.

OH, TELL ME, LARRY.... WHAT AM I MISSING?
Cat *VEESHUS*... Once eenside zeeba house, cat will **KEEL** heem! **KEEL** heem! ***KEEL*** heem!

ZZZZZZ
PURRRRRRRRRRRR

Pssst...Cat... Ees crocs... Does you keel zeeba?
TAP TAP TAP

Hsssssssssssss

Me popped heem.

Where is you running, Floyd?
Secret Agent Cat leave us special message! Me tink it say he keel zeeba!

Where he leave special message?!
He bury right here!...
DIG DIG DIG DIG DIG

Dat not very special.

10/4
HELLO... WELCOME TO 'DULLARD COMPUTER' TECH SUPPORT... PLEASE STAY ON THE LINE... YOUR CALL IS IMPORTANT TO US...

SO IMPORTANT, IN FACT, THAT WE'LL KEEP YOU ON HOLD FOR FOUR HOURS INSTEAD OF ACTUALLY HIRING PEOPLE WHO COULD TAKE YOUR CALL.

AAAAUGHH!
OHH YOU SAD POWERLESS LITTLE TROLL...

Hi. Welcome to 'Dullard' Computer's Tech Support Voice-Recognition System. Please state the problem you're having.
MY COMPUTER WON'T BOOT UP.

10/5
I'm sorry. I didn't get that. Please say your problem again.
MY... COMPUTER... WON'T... BOOT...

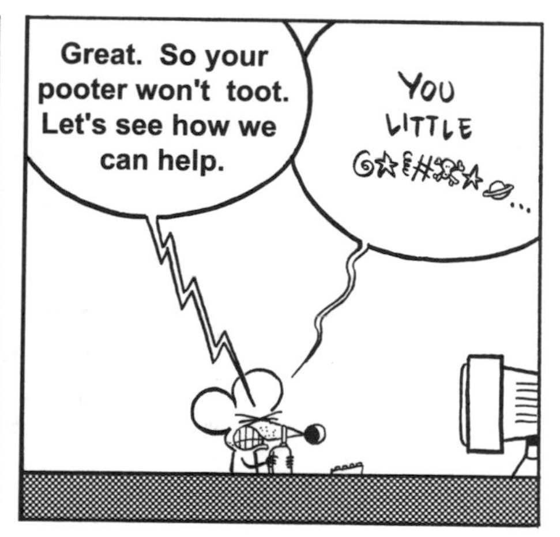
Great. So your pooter won't toot. Let's see how we can help.
YOU LITTLE

WHAT ARE YOU DOING NOW, RAT?
I'M PERFORMING A PUBLIC SERVICE... THE WORLD CRIES OUT FOR ME.
Dr. Rat's Brain Augmentation Surgery

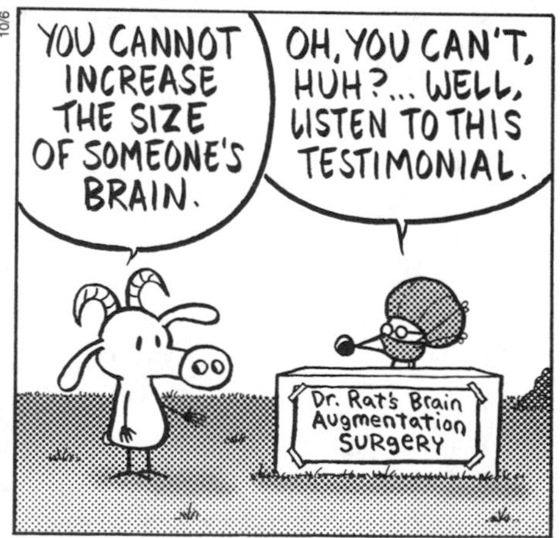
10/6
YOU CANNOT INCREASE THE SIZE OF SOMEONE'S BRAIN.
OH, YOU CAN'T, HUH?... WELL, LISTEN TO THIS TESTIMONIAL.
Dr. Rat's Brain Augmentation Surgery

I FEEL SMARTERERER THAN EVERER!
Dr. Rat's Brain Augmentation Surgery

Danny Donkey hated people.

They made him wait at the supermarket.

They made him wait at the video store.

They made him wait at the amusement park.

So Danny Donkey cut the line.
Cut the line at the supermarket.
Cut the line at the video store.
Cut the line at the amusement park.

Why, Danny Donkey cut every line he could find.

But for everything we do, there are consequences. And this was no exception. For as a result of all his line-cutting, Danny Donkey saw that he had become something he had never been before...

Happy.

WHAT ARE YOU DOING, PIG?
I'M FLYING TO A BIG CONVENTION THINGIE AND I'M TAKING ALONG MY VIKING FIGURINES.

TAKING YOUR VIKINGS, HUH? WHAT IS IT, A GUN SHOW? KNIFE SHOW?

LILAC FESTIVAL.
10/8

THERE'S A GUY WHO DOESN'T LIKE LILACS.

GATES 1 - 6
10/9

EXCUSE ME, SIR....IS THIS YOUR VIKING?
YES, OFFICER. WHAT'S GOING ON?

I CAUGHT HIM IN THE BATHROOM STALL TRYING TO RUB HIS FOOT AGAINST MINE.

I HAVE A WIDE STANCE.

THE VIKING SCANDAL
GOOD MORNING. I AM RAT. I HAVE BEEN RETAINED BY SVEN THE VIKING IN THIS MATTER.
10/10

MY CLIENT IS INNOCENT! INNOCENT! INNOCENT! INNOCENT! INNOCENT!
PSST

WHISPER WHISPER WHISPER WHISPER

MY CLIENT INFORMS ME THAT HE HAS IN FACT PLED GUILTY.

WHISPER WHISPER WHISPER WHISPER

I HAVE INFORMED MY CLIENT THAT HE HAS THE BRAINS OF A SEA SQUIRREL.

WHAT'S GOING ON, RAT?
SVEN THE VIKING IS RESIGNING FROM VIKINGDOM. IT'S HIS FAREWELL CEREMONY.

GOODBYE, SVEN, YE OF THE WIDE STANCE...YOU HAVE SHAMED VIKINGS EVERYWHERE... BE GONE WITH YE.

AS YE WISH, OLAF. BUT 'TIS A LONG JOURNEY... MAY I USE THE FACILITIES FIRST?
I SUPPOSE.

WHISPER WHISPER WHISPER
NO, YOU MAY NOT TAKE ALONG A BATHROOM BUDDY.

WHAT ARE YOU READING, DAD?
Ees high school yearbook. Me was Meester Beeg Man on Campus. Everyone respekk me. Dat's why dey all sign yearbook.

"DEAR LARRY...HOPE YOU HAVE A RADICAL SUMMER...TOO BAD YOU'RE TOO LAME TO CATCH A ZEBRA.... LOSER!"

Maybe he talking about deeferent Larry.

LOOK, RAT, I GOT US MATCHING "B.F.F." SHIRTS...."B.F.F." STANDS FOR "BEST FRIENDS FOREVER."... HAHAHA...WE CAN WEAR THEM TOGETHER.
GIMME THAT.

SCRIBBLE SCRIBBLE SCRIBBLE
WRITE WRITE WRITE

"I. D. K. T. F. G."?

"I DON'T KNOW THE FAT GUY."

HELLO THERE. CAN I HELP YOU?
YES... I'M LOOKING FOR A COLORFUL PAINTING FOR MY BEDROOM.
ART GALLERY

I SEE... WELL, THERE'S THIS ONE HERE. IT'S CALLED, 'THE FERRET'S ELF.'

OH, GEE, NO... THOSE COLORS ARE MUCH TOO FAIR... I'M LOOKING FOR SOMETHING WITH DARKER, RICHER COLORS... OH, WELL.. THANKS ANYWAYS.
10/14

WAIT WAIT WAIT... DON'T LEAVE... WE HAVE MANY PAINTINGS WITH DARKER HUES... I ASSURE YOU... THIS IS THE ONLY ONE LIKE THIS.
REALLY?

YES... THE ONLY THING WE HAVE TOO FAIR IS 'FERRET'S ELF.'

SAY YOUR PRAYERS, CARTOONIST BOY.
S. PASTIS

HEY THERE, GOAT...WHO ARE THESE GUYS?
MY NEW HAMSTERS, ORVILLE AND STEVE.
SQUEAK SQUEAK SQUEAK
10/15

STEVE RUNS IN HIS WHEEL ALL DAY. ORVILLE JUST TRIES TO NAP.
HOW CUTE...DON'T YOU WONDER WHAT GOES ON IN THEIR L'IL HAMSTER HEADS?
SQUEAK SQUEAK SQUEAK

KILL STEVE.
SQUEAK SQUEAK SQUEAK SQUEAK

GOAT'S HAMSTERS: ORVILLE AND STEVE
BEG YOUR PARDON, GOAT.. I DON'T MEAN TO BE A BOTHER, BUT I SIMPLY CANNOT CONCENTRATE WITH THE INFERNAL RACKET THAT IS STEVE.
SORRY, ORVILLE. I'VE ONLY GOT ONE CAGE.
SQUEAK SQUEAK SQUEAK SQUEAK
10/16

I SEE...WELL PERHAPS YOU COULD LET STEVE RUN FREE THROUGH THE NEIGHBORHOOD... HE SEEMS TO ENJOY THAT.
HE'D BE KILLED IN FIVE MINUTES.
SQUEAK SQUEAK SQUEAK

OH, DO HURRY.
SQUEAK SQUEAK SQUEAK

Dear Pigita, ♡
Please do not break up with me. I am a good boyfriend. I am strong. I am tough. I am brave.
10/17

DUDE, SHOW A LITTLE VULNERABILITY... CHICKS CAN'T RESIST A GUY WHO ADMITS HE HAS SOME WEAK SPOTS.

I have gas.

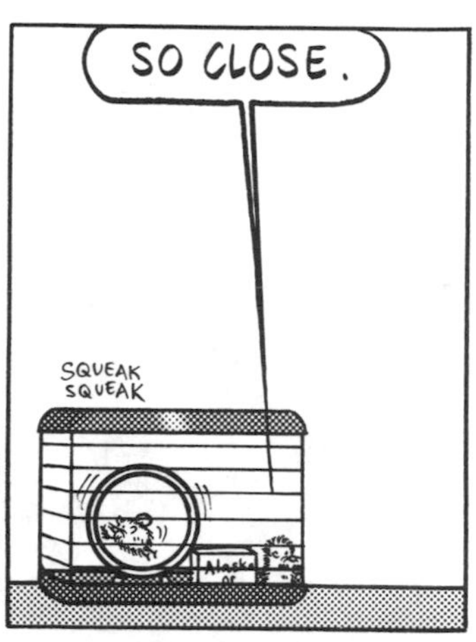

LISTEN, ORVILLE... I KNOW YOU'RE UPSET HAVING TO LIVE WITH STEVE AND HIS NOISY WHEEL, SO I BOUGHT YOU THIS L'IL TYPEWRITER. MAYBE BEING CREATIVE AND WRITING STORIES CAN HELP YOU INDULGE YOUR LITERARY PASSIONS.

I'M PLEASED YOU ASKED, BECAUSE I BELIEVE I HAVE A COMPROMISE THAT WILL BE ACCEPTABLE TO ALL.
GREAT. WHAT IS IT?
SHIP STEVE TO THE IDITAROD.
SQUEAK SQUEAK

SQUEAK SQUEAK SQUEAK SQUEAK

I hate Steve.
TYPE TYPE

WHAT ARE YOU READING, PIG?
A MAGAZINE. I LIKE TO STAY INFORMED ABOUT THE WAR IN IRAQ AND WHY WE'RE FIGHTING THERE.

WHAT MAGAZINE?
'SKY MALL.'

IT'S NOT SUPER INFORMATIVE.

Hey guys... What going on here?

Yo, dude..Just having some friends over for a barbecue. I'd invite you over, but I only have enough for them.
Hey... Dat is no probbum, dude.

That's the great part about being a predator, isn't it?... You can just go out and kill something for yourself, unlike those dumpy whiny humans who have to go to restaurants for their meat.

LOSER HUMANS
HA HA HA HA HA HA HA
HA HA
HA HA HA HA HA HA HA HA

CHOMP
CHOMP
CHOMP
CHOMP
CHOMP

WHAT ARE YOU DOING, RAT?
I AM A KING. THESE ARE MY PEOPLE. THEY LOOK TO ME FOR SAFETY AND SECURITY.
10/22

WHAP

I LIKE TO KEEP EXPECTATIONS LOW.

WHAT ARE YOU DOING, RAT?
I AM A KING. THESE ARE MY PEOPLE. THEY KNOW THAT UNDER ME, THEIR WELL-BEING IS ASSURED.

WHAT THEY DO NOT KNOW IS THAT TODAY IS 'WHIMSICAL TUESDAY,' WHEN BAD THINGS JUST HAPPEN.

KSSHH
10/23

'WHIMSICAL TUESDAYS' ARE A GOOD DAY TO STAY IN BED.

WHAT ARE YOU DOING NOW, RAT?
THIS IS BOB... BOB HAS CHOSEN TO LEAD AN INSURRECTION AGAINST MY RULE.
10/24

FOR THIS, HE WILL SLEEP WITH THE FISHES... AN EXAMPLE TO ALL....
PLOOP

IT'S HARD TO INTIMIDATE A PEOPLE WHO FLOAT.

NUTS! MY MOM'S COMING OVER IN FIVE MINUTES AND I FORGOT TO CLEAN UP MY STUFF.
RELAAAX, LITTLE BUDDY I GOT YOU COVERED.
10/25

SOMETIMES IT PAYS TO LIVE IN A COMIC STRIP.
I KINDA WANTED THAT SHOE.

HEY, RAT, LISTEN... PLEASE DON'T ERASE STUFF IN THE COMIC STRIP... IT SORTA DESTROYS THE ILLUSION THAT THIS IS ITS OWN QUASI-REAL WORLD.

THIS FROM THE GIGANTOHEAD EGOMANIAC WHO WALKS IN AND OUT OF HIS OWN COMIC STRIP?
HEY HEY HEY... WATCH WHO YOU'RE CALLING A GIGANTOHEAD EGO—
10/26

OHHHHH... NOW WAS THAT REALLY NECESSARY?
WHOA... BIG IMPROVEMENT.
IT'S OKAY, STEPHAN... HEADS ARE OVER-RATED.

WHAT ARE YOU DOING?
Me celebrating! Rumor is da crocs keel stoopid antylope across street! HAHAHA... In you face, wussy zeeba! WOOHOOHOO!!
Meeshunn AKKOMPISHED
10/27

WHAT'S ALL THE NOISE?
Meeshunn AKKOMPISHED

Sign not my idea.
Meeshunn AKKOMPISHED

ANYTHING?
NO.

IS THAT IT?
NOPE.

HOW 'BOUT NOW?
NOTHING.

ANYTHING?
NOPE.

GREAT PUMPKIN, MY FANNY.

WHAT'S THE MATTER WITH YOU GUYS?
Duuude... It's the ex-wives. They didn't make their support payment this week.

YOU MEAN THOSE FROZEN ZEBRAS THEY SHIP YOU?
Yep. And I'm ticked, bro. That's supposed to be on our front porch every Monday. I swear, when I find out what's going on, I'm gonna *kill* someone.
10/29

Me caught it. Me swear.
FROZEN ZEBRA

HEY THERE, MAX... I HEAR YOU STILL DIDN'T GET YOUR EX-WIFE'S SHIPMENT OF FROZEN ZEBRA... HOW YOU HANGING IN THERE?

10/30

THIS MIGHT BE A GOOD TIME TO TAKE A BREAK FROM OUR RELATIONSHIP.

TREECK OR TREET!
WHO ARE YOU SUPPOSED TO BE?

Me Gollum. From Lord of Reengs.
GOLLUM? WHY GOLLUM?
10/31

DA PRESHISS
AAAHHH

HEY THERE, ZEBRA... WE GONNA WATCH 'LITTLE MISS SUNSHINE'?
CAN'T. I HAVEN'T BEEN ABLE TO GET MY 'NETFLIX' MOVIES SINCE MAIL DELIVERY STOPPED.

WHAT HAPPENED TO YOUR MAIL?
DON'T KNOW... THE MAILMAN JUST STOPPED SHOWING UP... WE'RE ALL KINDA WONDERING WHAT HAPPENED TO HIM.
11/1

I could have done without the mace aperitif.

WHOA! WHO'S THAT UP THERE?
NUTS! IT'S TATA, THE WILLOWY TEMPTRESS O'TEMPTATION!

WHAT'S SHE DO?
SHE TRIES TO GET YOU TO FOLLOW HER, AND IF YOU'RE DUMB ENOUGH TO DO IT, SHE WRECKS YOU, RUINS YOU, AND REDUCES YOU TO A LIFE OF UNSPEAKABLE REGRET...
11/2

ADMITTEDLY, IT'S HARD TO EXPLAIN MY DECISION MAKING.

WHAT ARE YOU DOING UP THERE, RAT?
I'M BEING CARRIED OFF BY TATA, THE WILLOWY TEMPTRESS O' TEMPTATION!

SHE WILL WRECK ME, RUIN ME, REDUCE ME TO A WRETCHED PILE O' RUEFUL REGRET!
THEN WHY DON'T YOU JUST LET GO?
11/3

SHE SMELLS GOOD.

WOW... CAN YOU BELIEVE THIS STORY ?... THIS—

WHAT'D YOU SAY, GOAT?
OH, I WAS GOING TO TELL RAT SOMETHING BUT HE'S LISTENING TO MUSIC ON HIS IPOD.

OH, HE'S NOT LISTENING TO MUSIC... HE JUST WEARS THAT SO PEOPLE *THINK* HE'S LISTENING TO MUSIC. THEN THEY DON'T TALK TO HIM. AND THAT MAKES HIM HAPPY BECAUSE HE THINKS EVERY-ONE BUT HIM IS AN 'IDIOT FATHEAD.'

I DENY THAT.

Hey, dude. Thanks for inviting us over to your party.
Oh, no probbum, duuude.. We want welcome fellow predators to neigh-bahood... We is friends, no enemees.
Welcome

Hey, no worries, bro... What's this?
Oh... Dat is outdoor movie screen... We rent... But peese no touch curtain.
Welcome

Worries. We've got worries.
Me told you no touch curtain.
Welcome
FROZEN ZEBRA
BEER
11/5

Croc safehowse where we is live while we hyde from angree lions whose fud we steeled.

fehowse
e is live
e hyde
gree lions
fud we
led.

11/6

...CRUNCH CRUNCH CRUNCH CRUNCH CRUNCH...
Nice sign, bro.
Me speak gud croc.
CRUNCH
CRUNCH CRUNCH

LARRY... YOUR COUSIN DENA CALLED... THE LIONS ATE HER HUSBAND NICK LAST NIGHT... APPARENTLY, THEY THOUGHT HE WAS THE ONE WHO STOLE THE ZEBRA MEAT.
WOT?
YEAH, I GUESS SOMEONE XEROXED OFF THOUSANDS OF FLYERS CONTAINING A BOGUS 'CONFESSION' FROM NICK AND PUT THEM UP ALL OVER THE NEIGHBORHOOD.
WOT?
I'M NICK I DID IT
11/7

OH.. AND I FOUND A $200 KINKO'S RECEIPT IN YOUR POCKET.
WOT?

NUTS! THE COP BEHIND US IS PULLING ME OVER.
RELAX...I'LL HANDLE THIS.
RRRRR RRRRR RRRR
11/8

DO YOU HAVE ANY IDEA HOW FAST YOU WERE GOING?

NO, SIR, WE DON'T...AND BY THE SOUND OF YOUR QUESTION, I TAKE IT YOU DON'T EITHER.

HE KNEW MORE THAN HE WAS LETTING ON.

WHAT ARE YOU UP TO, GOAT?
I'M REMINDING THESE PEOPLE WHO POST ON MY BLOG TO STOP BEING SO PETTY.

BELIEVE IT OR NOT, THERE ARE SOME ANONYMOUS FOLK OUT THERE WHO SEE THE INTERNET AS NOTHING MORE THAN AN OUTLET FOR THEIR IMMATURE RANTS.
11/9

I know you are, but what am I?

Dear Pigita,
You are a good girlfrend.
I wish I was a good boyfrend. It's just that I get nervous around you.
I always think I'll screw up.

YOU STUPID PIG...CHICKS DON'T LIKE THAT...CHICKS LIKE GUYS WHO ARE CONFIDENT.

11/10
I always KNOW I'll screw up.

POP!

HOP!

11/11

HEY. I'M YOUR BRAIN. I'M LEAVING.
LEAVING? DON'T I NEED YOU?

NEED ME? ALL YOU DO IS WATCH 'AMERICAN IDOL' AND EAT CHEESE POOFS.
BUT WHERE WILL YOU GO? HOW WILL I FIND YOU?

YOU WON'T.
YOU MEAN...?

YOU'VE LOST YOUR MIND.

LET'S PLAY 'SCRABBLE' FOR CASH.

HI, GOAT... HAVE YOU MET MY BRAIN? HE GOT TIRED OF ME NOT USING HIM, SO HE LEFT MY HEAD.
SO THAT'S JUST EMPTY SPACE IN YOUR HEAD?

11/12

NO. RAT'S USING IT.
FOR?

MIND IF I GRAB ANOTHER BREWSKI?
GO FOR IT.
YO. HOOK A BROTHER UP WITH A COLD ONE.
I GIVE UP.
BEER

ALRIGHT... YOU'RE A BRAIN... YOU KNOW THE PRINCIPLES OF QUANTUM PHYSICS, NEUROSCIENCE AND MOLECULAR BIOLOGY... SO TELL ME. WHAT IS THE POINT OF LIFE?

TO DRINK BEER AND MEET WOMEN.
BEER

11/13

SUDDENLY, MY ENTIRE EXISTENCE HAS BEEN JUSTIFIED.
BEER

HEY, BABY... I'M A BRAIN... LET ME STUN YOU WITH MY MASSIVE HIPPOCAMPUS.
WHAT'S THAT?

11/14

THAT'S THE AREA OF THE BRAIN THAT CONTROLS MEMORY STORAGE.
WHATEVER.

DID I MENTION THAT I ALSO HAVE A BIG TRUCK AND A BAD ATTITUDE?

A SAD MOMENT FOR MY MASSIVE HIPPOCAMPUS.

HEY, RAT... WHAT ARE *YOU* DOING AT THIS JOB FAIR?
NETWORKING. I'M NO IDIOT. EVEN I KNOW THAT'S IMPORTANT.
B FAIR

THAT'S TERRIFIC... YOU'RE EVEN WEARING ONE OF THOSE NAME TAG STICKERS... LET'S SEE, IT SAYS, "HELLO, MY NAME IS..."
FAIR

"... NONE OF YOUR BUSINESS."
I'VE GOT MY LIMITATIONS.
FAIR
11/15

HEY, RAT... HAVE YOU SEEN MY BRAIN? HE TOOK OFF THIS MORNING AND I HAVEN'T SEEN HIM SINCE.
11/16

HE SAID HE WAS OFF TO MAKE SOME CASH.
MAKE CASH?... HOW?

PREPARE TO BE DOMINATED.
JEOPARDY!™
JUSTIN
Penny
The Brain

NO TRESPASSING GUARD DOG ON DUTY

HI, FELLAS. HEY, LISTEN, IF YOU DON'T MIND, I'D REALLY, REALLY APPRECIATE IT IF YOU COULD JUST MOVE A TEENSY BIT OVER THAT WAY.
11/17
NOT TODAY, TIMMY... I DON'T FEEL LIKE IT.
OH, OKAY... NO PROBLEMO... HEY, YOU HAVE YOURSELF A SUPER SPLENDIFOROUS DAY!!

...TIMMY THE GUARD DOG LEAVES SOMETHING TO BE DESIRED.

Danny Donkey loved his family.

Danny Donkey loved Thanksgiving.

But Danny Donkey did not love to see his family at Thanksgiving.

So every Thanksgiving, Danny grabbed half the turkey and locked himself in the bathroom.

Which was fine until it came time for the awkward toast...

To my family, who I can only love through a bathroom door.

Uncle Bob could also be a problem.

When Thanksgiving was over, Danny realized his self-imposed physical separation from his family had a consequence.

He loved them more.

YOU CALL THIS A CHILDREN'S THANKSGIVING TALE?
"CHAPTER TWO: THE DAY UNCLE BOB'S BLADDER WENT BOOM."
POOR UNCLE BOB.

Hulloo°oo leetle peeg.. How you like buy balloon for Nashanull Keel-A-Zeeba Day?
WHAT IS THAT?
Nashanull Keel-A-Zee Day!

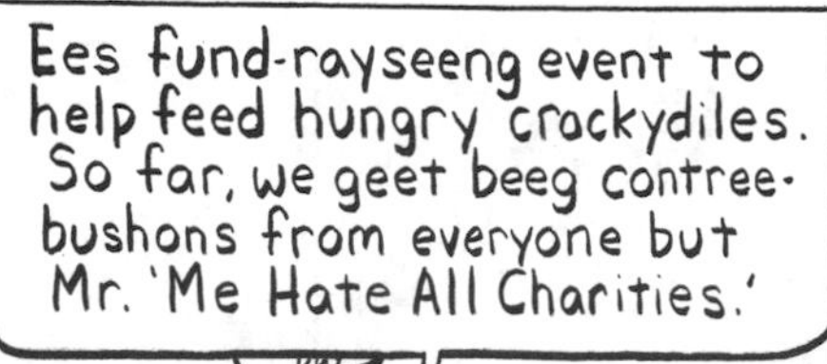
Ees fund-rayseeng event to help feed hungry crackydiles. So far, we geet beeg contree-bushons from everyone but Mr. 'Me Hate All Charities.'

I DO NOT HATE ALL CHARITIES.
Mebbe he juss super cheep.
Nashanull Keel-A-Zee Day!

I CAN'T BELIEVE THOSE CROCS THINK THEY CAN RAISE MONEY BY SELL-ING BALLOONS TO MY FRIENDS FOR 'NATIONAL KEEL-A-ZEBRA DAY.'
DON'T WORRY, ZEBRA... IT'LL NEVER WORK.

Nashanull Keel-A-Zee Day!

SO I LIKE BALLOONS.
Nashanull Keel-A-Zee Day!

Hey, Meester Beeg Cat...Me hear you eat mailman... How you do it?

How do you mean, bro? It's just a slow, dumpy human. It's like catching a rutabaga.

How you catch rutabaga?

Okaaay, zeeba neighba... Me is strapped to you tree. If you no agree to demands, me and you ees both blow up in two minute.
TICK TICK TICK
TICK TICK

I'M NOT STRAPPED TO THE TREE. YOU'RE STRAPPED TO THE TREE. I CAN JUST WALK AWAY AND WATCH YOU EXPLODE.
TICK TICK
TICK TICK

TICK TICK
TICK TICK
TICK TICK

Touché.
TICK TICK
TICK TICK

HEY, RAT... BOY, DO I HAVE A STORY TO TELL YOU!
FINE. BUT BEFORE YOU DO, I NEED TO SAY SOMETHING.

WHAT'S THAT?
THIS CONVERSATION MAY BE MONITORED FOR QUALITY ASSURANCE PURPOSES.

MAYBE I'LL JUST BE QUIET.
A WISE CHOICE.

I SAW CAROL YESTERDAY. SHE SAID ED KILLED A ZEBRA.
Right... Like me believe DAT...Me happen know Ed buy dat from store.

IS THAT SO?...TELL ME, LARRY, WHAT STORE SELLS DEAD ZEBRAS? HUH?...TELL ME, LARRY.

FLIIIIIIIIP....
YELLOW PAGES
PICK

"Payless Shoes."

...LIE AGAIN, LARRY... I DARE YOU!
Wait wait.... "Betty's Bridal Emporium." No no....

GOODBYE. I'M LEAVING. FOR REAL THIS TIME.
WHERE YOU GOING, MY LITTLE BRAIN?

CLUB BRAIN. IT'S A BIG RESORT...REAL POPULAR WITH BRAINS.
THERE ARE MORE OF YOU ESCAPED BRAINS RUNNING AROUND?

YES. WE TEND TO ESCAPE DURING PROLONGED PERIODS OF TELEVISION VIEWING... MOST PEOPLE DON'T EVEN NOTICE WE'RE GONE.
HOW MANY OF YOU HAVE FLED LIKE THAT?

11/25

IF YOU MUST KNOW, THIRTY-FOUR PERCENT OF ALL PEOPLE ARE WALKING AROUND WITHOUT A BRAIN.

TOODLES.

EXPLAINS A LOT.

AND THIS IS VICTORIA, BRITISH COLUMBIA.. ISN'T IT PRETTY? ONE DAY I'LL GO THERE...BUT FIRST I WANT TO SEE AFRICA... NO, FIRST I WANT TO SEE INDIA... BEAUTIFUL, MYSTICAL INDIA .

DO YOU THINK I'LL HAVE ANY TROUBLE GETTING THERE, PIG ?

11/26

NOT THAT I CAN THINK OF, ANDY.
GOOD.. BECAUSE I WAS A LITTLE WORRIED ABOUT SPECIAL VISA REQUIREMENTS.

HEY, PIG.. MIND BUYING ME A BOTTLE OF SUN-BLOCK FOR MY CRUISE TO TRINIDAD ?
WHEN ARE YOU TAKING A CRUISE TO TRINIDAD, ANDY?
11/27

NEXT WEEK.
BUT.... ...HOW ?

THE CRUISE LINE USUALLY PROVIDES A BOAT.

OH... RIGHT.
I WORRY ABOUT YOU, PIG .

HEY, GOAT, YOU WRITING YOUR BLOG ?
GO AWAY, RAT.
11/28

YOU KNOW, I LIKE BLOGS... I REALLY DO... YOU KNOW WHY?
GO AWAY, RAT.

BECAUSE THEY PROVIDE THEIR FRUS-TRATED CREATOR WITH THE DELUSIONAL OUTLET OF BEING A PUBLISHED AUTHOR. SORT OF LIKE HOW THE PRISON WAR-DEN LETS THE PSYCHOTIC INMATE SCRIBBLE 'POETRY' ON THE CELL WALL SO HE DOESN'T BEAT HIS BUNK MATE WITH A TOILET SEAT.

PERHAPS YOU DIDN'T LIKE THE ANALOGY.

Okay, zeeba neighba, leesten me. Crocs get costume deepartment. Now we look inteemidating! See, me is Skullhead Doom Guy!!

And me is ballerina!

Back to costume deepartment, Bob.

THAT STUPID LITTLE DOG FRIEND OF YOURS ASKED ME TO BUY HIM A PANAMA HAT FOR SOME CRUISE HE'S TAKING TO TRINIDAD.
POOR ANDY. HE DOESN'T SEEM TO KNOW HE'S ATTACHED TO A CHAIN.

YEAH... WHAT AM I SUPPOSED TO DO? BUY HIM A HAT HE CAN'T BUY FOR HIMSELF JUST TO ENCOURAGE SOME IMPOSSIBLE DREAM?
I KNOW. IT'S SO HARD... SO WHAT DID YOU DO?

OHH, ANDY... YOU MISSED YOUR CRUISE.
I KNOW... I WALKED ALL NIGHT, BUT I DIDN'T GET ANYWHERE.

AWWWW ANDY... IT'S... IT'S... BECAUSE YOU'RE—
...ON A CHAIN. A CHAIN THAT GETS A LITTLE WEAKER EVERY TIME I PULL AGAINST IT... A CHAIN THAT ONE DAY'S GONNA BREAK.

OH, ANDY...
HEY... DON'T SQUISH THE HAT.

HOW COME WE ALWAYS HAVE TO COME TO THIS EXPENSIVE TREE LOT, RAT?
BECAUSE THAT CUTE GIRL WORKS HERE AND I WANT TO ASK HER OUT.
12/2

OHH, I REMEMBER HER FROM LAST CHRISTMAS. SHE MAKES YOU *NERVOUS*.
SHUT UP. JUST SHUT UP.

OOOOH... SHE'S WALKING OVER.
DUDE DUDE DUDE... DON'T @☆#@☆#@ *STARE*.

WHAT SHOULD I DO?
JUST BE A NORMAL WINGMAN, YOU IDIOT. WATCH MY BACK. DON'T LET ME GO DOWN IN FLAMES.

CAN I HELP YOU?
Yes. Hello. Good evening. I am of interest in buying a Christmas home for my tree room living.

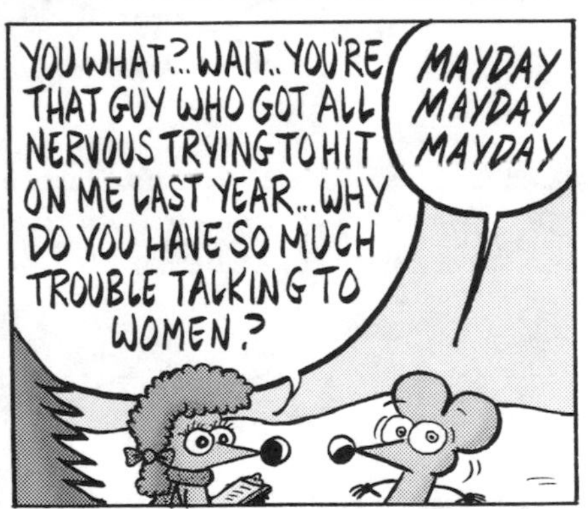
YOU WHAT?.. WAIT.. YOU'RE THAT GUY WHO GOT ALL NERVOUS TRYING TO HIT ON ME LAST YEAR... WHY DO YOU HAVE SO MUCH TROUBLE TALKING TO WOMEN?
MAYDAY MAYDAY MAYDAY

BECAUSE HE'S SPENT A LIFETIME IN MEN'S PRISON!!!

...OH...THAT WAS SMOOTH.
WAIT... SHE'S COMING BACK... NO, THAT'S A COP.

WHY ARE YOU TAKING SO LONG IN THE BATHROOM, RAT?
I'M GETTING DRESSED FOR MY BIG DATE WITH THE GIRL FROM THE CHRISTMAS TREE LOT.

SHE AGREED TO GO OUT WITH YOU?
YES, BUT IT TOOK WORK, AND I DON'T WANT TO BLOW IT... SO I'M GETTING ALL DRESSED UP AND TAKING HER SOMEWHERE FANCY.

ARE YOU WEARING YOUR GOOD SHOES?
I CAN'T FIND THE STUPID THINGS... ALL I CAN FIND ARE MY WORK SHOES.
WORK SHOES? FROM WHEN YOU....

...DRESSED AS A CLOWN FOR THE PARTY SUPPLY STORE?
LAUGH AND I STOMP YOUR HEAD.
12/3

THANKS FOR MEETING ME HERE, CHRISTMAS TREE GIRL.
YOU'RE WELCOME. BUT I HAVE TO GET BACK TO WORK IN — ... WHAT'S THAT HITTING ME UNDER THE TABLE?

SHOES.
WHY ARE YOU WEARING CLOWN SHOES?
12/4

I am a big fan of clowns. Big fan. Big, big fan. It is my homage to —
SQUEEZE SQUEEZE

WHAT WAS THAT?
I WANTED TO SEE IF YOUR NOSE HONKED.

THIS IS A NICE PLACE.

It is. Of niceness. Yes.
YOU KNOW... WHY DO YOU GET SO NERVOUS WHEN YOU TALK TO ME?
12/5

BECAUSE YOU KEEP STARING INTO MY EYES LIKE YOU CAN SEE STRAIGHT INTO ME AND THAT WORRIES ME BECAUSE IT'S NOT A NICE PLACE IN THERE.
WHAT DO YOU WANT ME TO DO?

PLEASE TAKE YOUR NAPKIN OFF MY HEAD.

WHAT ARE YOU DOING, RAT?
I AM NOT RAT. I AM EGO-MAN, HERE TO INTRODUCE MY NEW SIDEKICK.
12/6

CAPTAIN TOO-FAT-TO-BE-OF-ASSISTANCE-BOY.

I DIDN'T PICK THE NAME.

BEHOLD! IT IS I, EGO-MAN, AND MY CRIMEFIGHTING ASSISTANT, CAPTAIN TOO-FAT-TO-BE-OF-ASSISTANCE BOY!!
GADZOOKS!
12/7

SO WHAT'S YOUR SIDEKICK DO TO FIGHT CRIME?
HE STANDS THERE AND YELLS 'GADZOOKS.'

EVERY LITTLE BIT HELPS.

WELL, SIR, I CONTINUE MY PUSH TO RID OUR NEIGHBORHOOD OF HOLIDAY INSURGENTS.
WHAT'S A HOLIDAY INSURGENT?

SCUM, SIR...TROUBLEMAKERS...NEIGHBORS WHO DISRUPT OUR OTHERWISE HARMONIOUS CHRISTMAS AESTHETIC WITH TACKY DECORATIONS.
WHO DOES THAT?
12/8

NEIGHBOR BOB, SIR. HE INSISTS ON DECORATING HIS FRONT LAWN WITH THOSE LIGHTED REINDEER WHOSE HEADS BOB UP AND DOWN...HE HAS TWO OF THEM.
I THINK HE HAS THREE.

TWO.

WELCOME TO
CLUB BRAIN
'WHERE THE MINDS UNWIND'
YO.. CHECK OUT THE CEREBELLUMS ON THOSE BABES... LET'S FOLLOW THEM, BOB....

..HEEEEEY THERE, LADIES... WANNA SEE A HUGE HYPOTHALAMUS?
GO AWAY, CREEP.

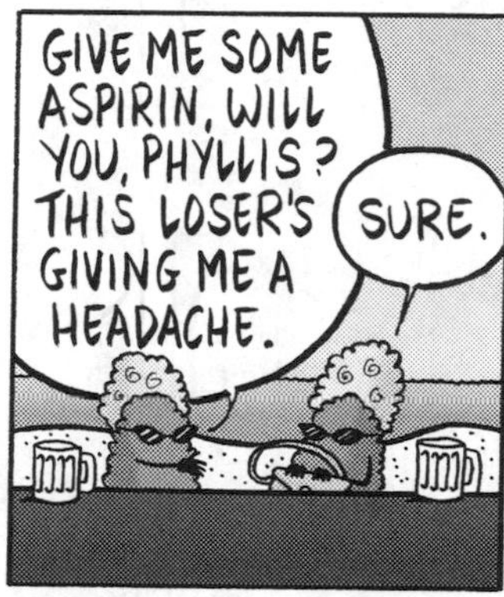
GIVE ME SOME ASPIRIN, WILL YOU, PHYLLIS? THIS LOSER'S GIVING ME A HEADACHE.
SURE.

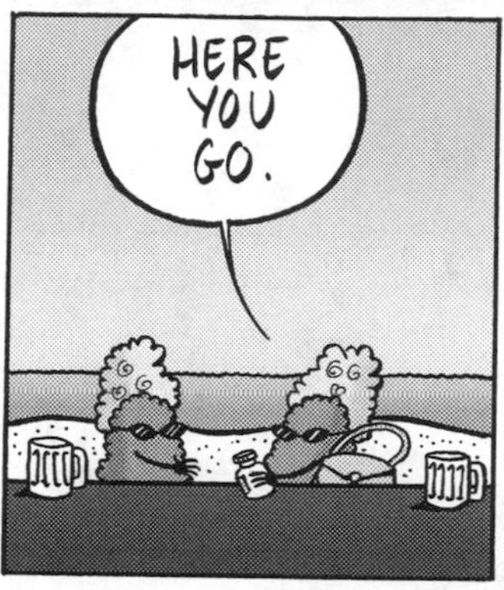
HERE YOU GO.

HEY HEY HEY
WHAT?!

THIS IS YOUR BRAIN.

THIS IS YOUR BRAIN ON DRUGS.

YOU WILL NEVER HEAR A BETTER PICK-UP LINE.

"Dear Mom and Dad, If I cannot have my zeeba girlfriend over for Chreesmas dinner, I cannot be dere eeder."

OHMYGAND!! MY SON HAS RUN AWAY! HE COULD BE ANYWHERE IN THE WORLD BY NOW!! HE COULD BE ON THE STREETS! COLD! STARVING!! ALONE!!

C-O-O-O-ME dey tell me, PAH RUMP PUM PUM PUMM
WELL... JUNIOR'S AGREED TO COME BACK HOME FOR CHRISTMAS DINNER... BUT ON ONE CONDITION... HE GETS TO BRING THAT ZEBRA'S ENTIRE FAMILY.
Merry ristmas

Gud. Me set Chreesmas trap!
CHRISTMAS TRAP, LARRY?
12/13

DAD! WHAT ARE YOU DOING?!
Me want smash zeeba over hed. Bah humbug.

YOU OUGHT TO BE ASHAMED OF YOURSELF DAD, DRESSING UP AS JOSEPH TO DO A SURPRISE ATTACK.. CAN A CROCODILE ACT ANY MORE SHAMEFULLY?
12/14

Is zeebas here yet?

WHAT'S WRONG WITH RAT?
HE'S BECOME A 'BLACKBERRY' FIEND. HE SENDS OUT E-MAIL DAY AND NIGHT.

IN FACT, I HAD TO GET MY OWN BECAUSE IT'S NOW THE ONLY WAY TO STILL COMMUNICATE WITH HIM.
BUT THAT'S NUTS.
12/15

TYPITY TYPITY TYPITY TYPE

Bite me.

RAT, EVER SINCE YOU GOT THAT 'BLACKBERRY,' IT'S ALL YOU DO.

I MEAN, I LIKE YOU, BUT I DON'T LIKE HAVING TO OWN MY OWN 'BLACKBERRY' JUST TO COMMUNICATE WITH YOU.

TYPITY
TYPE
TYPE

Why is that?
12/16

IT'S RUDE. AND IT'S IMPERSONAL. I LIKE *PERSONAL* CONTACT...

PAT
PAT
PAT
PAT

There, there.

THE CROC/ZEBRA CHRISTMAS DINNER
AS A SMALL THANKS FOR INVITING US OVER, WE ZEBRAS WANTED TO GIVE YOU THIS... A SYMBOLIC KEY TO OUR DOOR, REPRESENTING HOW YOU NOW VIEW US ZEBRAS AS REAL FRIENDS.

YES, WELL, THIS WAS REALLY JUNIOR'S IDEA, BUT THANKS.. AND I BELIEVE MY HUSBAND LARRY HAS A PRESENT FOR YOU...
12/17

Zeebas is FUD.
THE WINE, LARRY... THE WINE.
Hope you likes posters.

THE CROC/ZEBRA CHRISTMAS DINNER
THANKS SO MUCH FOR INVITING US OVER. IT'S BEEN A TOUGH YEAR FOR ME... LOT OF HEALTH ISSUES... GAINED A LOT OF WEIGHT... HARD FOR ME TO MOVE AROUND NOW....

Eat me. Eat me. Eat me. Eat me.
12/18

I'M FEELING UNCOMFORTABLE.

THE CROC/ZEBRA CHRISTMAS DINNER
IT'S SO WONDERFUL TO SEE OUR FAMILIES GETTING ALONG.
I KNOW... AND IT WAS SO NICE OF YOUR FAMILY TO GIVE MY MOM AND DAD THAT 'KEY OF FRIENDSHIP.'

WELL... SYMBOLS CAN BE IMPORTANT.
YEAH... AND I JUST KNOW THAT KEY WILL LEAD TO A WHOLE NEW LEVEL OF INTERACTION BETWEEN OUR FAMILIES...
12/19

WHAM
WHAM
WHAM

GEE..THIS ALL LOOKS GREAT! SHOULD WE SAY GRACE BEFORE WE EAT?
SURE... WAIT... WHERE'S UNCLE PETER?
I THOUGHT HE WAS WITH MY—

DAD.

12/20
OHHH... THIS IS A HEARTWARMING CHRISTMAS STORY.
GET SOME HELP, STEPH.
S. PASTIS

DAD! YOU KILLED ZEBRA'S UNCLE! HOW COULD YOU??
No, son, no... Is bucket of 'KFC.' Me realized keesmas about love. And peace. And brudderhood.

HE REALIZED THAT AFTER HE KNOCKED ME UNCONSCIOUS, HE COULDN'T DRAG ME ONTO THE BARBECUE BECAUSE I WAS TOO FAT. THAT, OF COURSE, DIDN'T STOP HIM FROM EATING PART OF MY LEFT LEG.
12/21

Way to bring down mood, Stumpy.

I'M SO SORRY MY DAD ATE YOUR UNCLE'S LEG, JOY..HE RUINED CHRISTMAS.
IT'S OKAY. MAYBE WE COULD ALL JUST SING SOME CHRISTMAS CAROLS TOGETHER. THAT WOULD END IT NICELY...
12/22

Jeengle bells
Zeebas smell
Uncle Pete lose leg.
Da croc-o-dile
Eat leg while
Pete hop on stump
all day.
CAROLS FOR CROCS

NEVER MIND.

BECAUSE THE AIRLINE SAYS HE CAN. AND THAT'S 'AIRPLANESEATRECLINEOLOGY.'.. PEOPLE WILL DO WHAT THEY ***CAN***, REGARDLESS OF ITS EFFECT ON OTHERS. AND THAT'S WHY THE WORLD IS IN THE STATE IT'S IN.

BEER

MERRY CHRISTMAS, PIGITA!
WHAT IS THAT HANGING FROM YOUR EARS?
12/24

SCENTED AIR FRESHENERS... I ALWAYS LIKE TO SMELL MY BEST.
THOSE ARE FOR YOUR CAR, YOU IDIOT... THEY'RE NOT SOMETHING YOU WEAR.

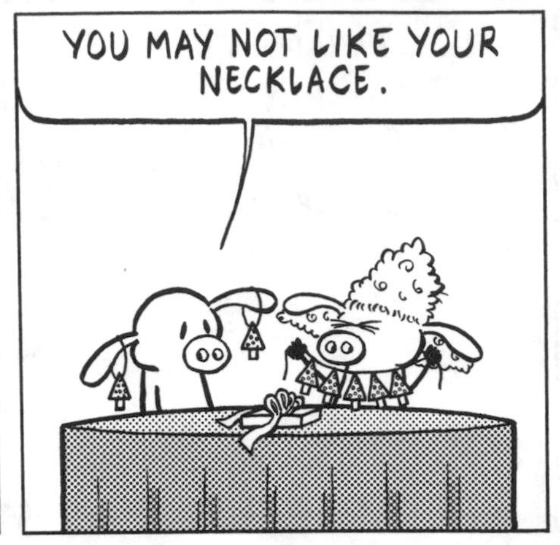
YOU MAY NOT LIKE YOUR NECKLACE.

I DIDN'T LIKE THE WAY THE CROC STORY ENDED, STEPHAN... I LIKE THE ENDINGS OF CHRISTMAS STORIES TO MAKE ME FEEL WARM AND HAPPY AND NICE.
HMM. WHAT DO YOU HAVE IN MIND, PIG?
S. PASTIS

WHISPER
WHISPER
WHISPER

OKAY... JUST FOR YOU, PIG.
12/25

'FEAR NOT, FOR BEHOLD, I BRING YOU TIDINGS OF GREAT JOY... FOR UNTO YOU IS BORN THIS DAY IN THE CITY OF DAVID, A SAVIOR.'

DON'T YOU THINK IT'S WEIRD HOW DURING ALL THE ROMAN WARS, THE SOLDIERS GOT DRESSED UP?
THEY DIDN'T GET DRESSED UP. WHAT ARE YOU TALKING ABOUT?
ROME
12/26

YEAH, IT SAYS RIGHT HERE THAT AFTER THE BATTLE OF CARTHAGE, THE FIELD WAS FILLED WITH ALL THESE CASUAL TIES.
'CASUALTIES.'

HISTORY IS SO CONFUSING.

WHO'S THAT SITTING NEXT TO YOU, RAT?
PABLO, THE DRUG-SNIFFING DOG.

OHH... THOSE DOGS ARE AMAZING! WHAT POLICE AGENCY DOES HE WORK WITH?

POLICE AGENCY?
OOOOOOOOH... LOOK AT THE FLYING MONKEYS...

HELLO THERE, MISTER.... I DON'T BELIEVE WE'VE MET...
Bzzzzzzz Bzzzzzz Bzzz Bzzzzzz

DO YOU TALK?
WHAT'S THE MATTER WITH YOU, PAL?... CAN'T YOU SEE THAT'S A BEE? WHAT BEE DO YOU KNOW THAT TALKS?

LIVING IN A COMIC STRIP CAN BE VERY CONFUSING.
Bzzzz Bzzzzz
...I TELL YOU, FLOYD, THE IDIOTS IN THIS PLACE ARE REALLY GETTING TO ME.
AWW, FORGET ABOUT IT, LARRY. ... HE'S JUST A DUMB PIG.

DO YOU EVER LOOK DOWN AT YOUR ALPHABET SOUP AND SEE ACTUAL WORDS?
YEAH, BUT THAT'S JUST WHAT HAPPENS WHEN YOU PUT RANDOM LETTERS TOGETHER. IT'S THE LAW OF PROBABILITIES.

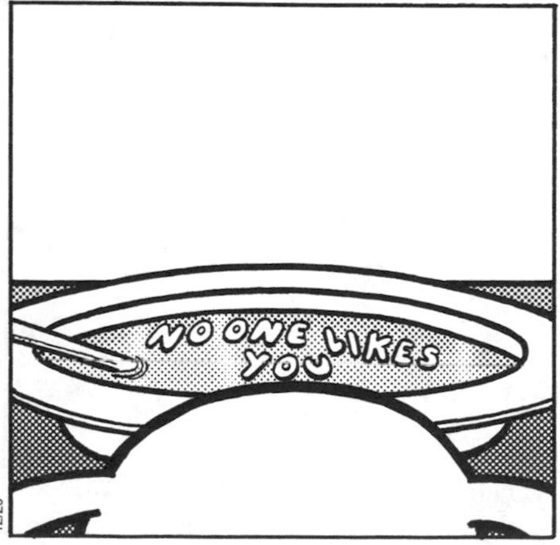
NO ONE LIKES YOU

THAT'S GOOD TO KNOW.

YOU READY FOR OUR VACATION, PIGITA?
GOT THE TICKETS, THE SUNSCREEN... WAIT... THE FIGHT... WHAT ARE WE GONNA FIGHT ABOUT?

I DUNNO.
WELL, WE HAVE TO FIGHT... IT'S VACATION... HERE, PICK A CARD FROM THE FIGHT BOX.
The Fight Box

"I WANT TO STRUCTURE EVERY MINUTE OF THE VACATION AND YOU DON'T."... NOT BAD, BUT TRY ANOTHER...
The Fight Box

"I'M NOT USED TO SPENDING THIS MUCH TIME WITH YOU AND YOU'RE SORTA GETTING ON MY NERVES."... PRETTY GOOD... BUT TRY ONE MORE...

"YOU PICKED THIS PLACE AND I DIDN'T, SO I'LL SUBTLY TRY TO MAKE YOU FEEL GUILTY ABOUT IT."... A *CLASSIC!!* LET'S PICK IT!

OKAY FINE, BUT LET'S HURRY... I'VE BEEN WANTING TO GO TO MAUI MY WHOLE LIFE! ISN'T IT INCREDIBLE TO THINK WE'RE ***REALLY*** GOING?

OH. SO INCREDIBLE.

WELL, HELLO, MA'AM... YOU'RE QUITE ATTRACTIVE. DO YOU FIND ME ATTRACTIVE?
NO.

SIMON SAYS FIND ME ATTRACTIVE.

SIMON SAYS BUY ME ANOTHER BEER.

I HEARD SOME FEMALE LIONS ARE VISITING YOU TODAY.
Yep. Me and Max are back on the market, so we want to look our best.

WHAT'S A FEMALE LION ATTRACTED TO?
Manes, mostly. The bigger the mane, the more likely the female is to see you as dominant.

Enough with the blow dryer, Max.

SO HAVE YOU AND MAX HAD ANY LUCK MEETING LADIES?
Nope... Our manes weren't big enough.

AREN'T FEMALE LIONS ATTRACTED TO ANYTHING OTHER THAN MANE SIZE?
Well, there's the loudness of your roar, but there's not much you can do about that. Either you got it or you don't.

You're really getting on my nerves, Max.

WHERE ARE *YOU* GOING?
I GOT AN E-MAIL FROM A DEPOSED NIGERIAN KING. HE NEEDS MY HELP CASHING A SIXTEEN MILLION DOLLAR CHECK. I'M GOING TO MEET HIM NOW. I'VE HIT THE BIG TIME.

THAT'S A SCAM, PIG. THEY STEAL YOUR MONEY.

YOU SOUND JEALOUS.
1/3

HAVE YOU AND MAX MET ANY FEMALE LIONS?
Nada, bro... Manes weren't big enough. Roars weren't loud enough.

WHAT'S LEFT?
Physical size, I guess. But what can I do about that?
1/4

Cool it with the 'roids, Max.

I'M A BAD LISTENER.
HOW SO?

I ONLY HEAR THINGS I WANT TO HEAR AND DISREGARD THE REST.
OHH, THAT'S NOT A GOOD WAY TO BE...HAVE YOU THOUGHT ABOUT TRYING TO CHANGE?
1/5

OoOookay, zeeba neighba... Now you had it. Dis is all-powerful, all-loving Box God. We pray to heem. He hate you.

IS THAT SO ?
Yes! Me juss ask and he kill you face! So geev up now!

I DON'T BELIEVE IN YOUR BOX GOD.
Whuuuh? Is you STOOpid? Now you so dead, it not even *funny!*.. Oh, let us PRAY....

Ohhh, all-powerful Box God.. ARISE and show you is all-powerful Box God of revengeness by chanting you War Song O' FURIOUS death.

♫ I love you...You love me ... ♪ We a happy fam-i-ly ♪

Dat wasn't right song, Bob.
Me get dem confused.

WHAT HAPPENED TO YOU?
REMORA. THEY'RE THOSE LITTLE FISH THAT STICK TO SHARKS AND MANTA RAYS AND STUFF.

THOSE ANIMALS LIVE IN THE WATER.

I TAKE VERY LONG SHOWERS.
1/7

I CAN'T BELIEVE YOU GOT REMORA FROM A LONG SHOWER.
IT WAS A VERY LONG SHOWER.

HOW YOU GONNA GET THOSE STUPID THINGS OFF?
I DON'T KNOW. I TRIED EVERYTHING. ALL I KNOW IS IT'S GONNA TAKE SOMETHING WITH A LOT OF FORCE.
1/8

HOLD STILL. REAL STILL.

EVERYWHERE I GO, I WANT TO TELL PEOPLE ABOUT THE IMPORTANCE OF CAMPAIGN FINANCE REFORM, BUT NO ONE LISTENS.
YEAH.. DON'T BOTHER, DUDE. IT'S LIKE CASTING PEARLS BEFORE SWINE.
1/9

HONK
HONK
CLAP
CLAP
CLAP
PEARLS BEFORE SWINE

THAT WAS ODD.

HI, MOM... NO, PIG'S NOT HERE YET... I DON'T KNOW IF HE'S GONNA ASK ME TO MARRY HIM... I'M JUST ASSUMING...

I MEAN, WHY ELSE WOULD HE CALL ME AN HOUR BEFORE OUR DINNER DATE AND TELL ME TO EXPECT SOMETHING DIFFERENT AND SPECIAL...

I'VE GOT TO GO, MOM.

I'VE REACHED A CONCLUSION... I HATE THE WORLD.
IS THAT SO?

YES, BUT WHEN I'M DRUNK, I **LOVE** THE WORLD.
AND THIS MEANS ?

THAT MY GETTING TOASTED IS A SELFLESS ACT OF KINDNESS.

YOU COULD AT LEAST BUY THE BEER.

SOMETIMES I LOOK UP AT THE SKY AND WONDER IF ANYTHING I EVER ACCOMPLISH IN LIFE WILL HAVE ANY SIGNIFICANCE.

SOMETIMES I LOOK UP AT THE SKY AND GET HIT BY BIRD DROPPINGS.

FRIENDS LIKE US HAVE LOTS IN COMMON.

Oh no. Someone has shot Bob the Croc. Larry the Croc insists it couldn't have been him because he was home watching TV. Why does Slylock not believe him?

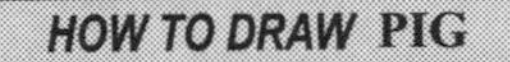

HOW TO DRAW PIG

1/13

YOUR DRAWING

This drawing of a tree was submitted by Jerry Scott of Malibu, CA

Which one of these comics was around when Hitler invaded Poland?

a) Blondie
b) Barney Google
c) Prince Valiant
d) Mary Worth
e) All of the above

ANSWER: (e)

APOLOGIES TO THE GREAT BOB WEBER, JR.

Can you find at least 6 differences between these panels?

PANEL 1

PANEL 2

1) First panel labeled "PANEL 1." Second panel labeled "PANEL 2"; 2) In Panel 1, Rat feels an internal urge to punch Pig. In Panel 2, urge is diminished; 3) Panel 2 is below Panel 1; 4) There is a flying toaster in Panel 2; 5 and 6) There are no fifth and sixth differences. The question asked was, "Can you find at least 6 differences?" The answer was no.

HEY, LOOK! A D.V.D. OF 'THE OFFICE'! THAT'S MY FAVORITE SHOW!
DON'T TOUCH IT, PIG... IT'S THE ROOF FISH... THEY'RE TRYING TO KILL YOU.

THE ROOF FISH?
THEY SIT ATOP THE PANEL AND TRY TO CATCH YOU USING THINGS THEY KNOW TEMPT YOU. IF YOU FALL FOR IT, THEY EAT YOU.

SO MUCH FOR OUR BACON BREAKFAST.

HEY, PIG...GET ME A BEER...I DON'T WANT TO MISS THIS PART.
I DON'T WANT TO MISS IT EITHER.

CURSE THOSE ROOF FISH.

HEY, NEIGHBOR GEORGE... WHAT'S WRONG?
I GOTTA MEET MY MOTHER HERE FOR LUNCH AND IT BUMS ME OUT. SHE'S GETTING OLD AND SHE'S ALWAYS COMPLAINING...SHE'S VERY NEGATIVE.

WHAT DOES SHE COMPLAIN ABOUT?
LATELY, IT'S THE FACT THAT HER SPINE IS COMPRESSING. IT HAPPENS SOMETIMES WHEN YOU GET OLDER AND YOUR BONES LOSE THEIR DENSITY. THAT'S WHY OLDER PEOPLE SOMETIMES LOSE SOME OF THEIR HEIGHT.

THAT DOESN'T SOUND TOO BAD. I BET SHE'LL BE FINE.
EASY FOR YOU TO SAY.

PIG, WE'VE BEEN GOING OUT FOR SIX YEARS...EITHER YOU GIVE ME A RING OR WE'RE FINISHED.
1/17

OH, PIG! IT'S BEAUTIFUL!

HOOKED A FAT ONE.
BEER

MY PROBLEM IN LIFE IS THAT WHENEVER SOMETHING GOOD HAPPENS TO ME, I ALWAYS FEAR THAT SOMETHING BAD WILL FOLLOW. SO I CAN NEVER ENJOY ANY OF MY SUCCESS.

YEAH. I KNOW WHAT YOU MEAN. I CAN NEVER ENJOY MY SUCCESS EITHER.
WHY IS THAT?
1/18

I DON'T HAVE ANY.

MAN, I'D LOVE TO TALK TO THAT HOT CHICK ON THE OTHER SIDE OF ME, BUT SHE'S CLEARLY ONE OF THOSE PRIM AND PROPER TYPES.

TRY A LITTLE HUMOR... WOMEN LOVE A GUY WHO CAN DEMONSTRATE A SUBTLE WIT.
HOW OBVIOUS. WHY DIDN'T I THINK OF THAT? ALRIGHT, PAL, HERE I GO....
1/19

YO...PULL MY FINGER.

Zeeba neighba! Zeeba neighba! Come QUEEK! Ees Jeemy Heinreeks FREE een CONCERT!

IT'S JIMI *HENDRIX*... AND HE'S DEAD. AND HE DIDN'T PLAY THE UKULELE.
1/20

WOT? He no beleeve me is Jeemy? Is he stoopid??
Prove to heem, Jeemy... Burn geetar! Burn geetar!
LIGHTER FLUID

SQUIRT

FFFFT

FOOSH

And da wind cry moron.
Me not feel great, Bob.

DO YOU THINK IT WOULD BE WRONG TO ATTEND A COMPLETE STRANGER'S FUNERAL JUST TO GET THE FREE FOOD?

OF COURSE IT'D BE WRONG. WHY WOULD YOU EVEN ASK?

I SURE DO MISS AL.
BOB.
OH.
R.I.P. BOB

RAT ATTENDS A STRANGER'S FUNERAL TO GET THE FREE FOOD.
I'M SORRY, SIR... WERE YOU A FRIEND OF BOB'S? I'VE NEVER MET YOU.
UH, YEAH... WE WORKED TOGETHER.
R.I.P. BOB

BOB NEVER HELD A JOB IN HIS LIFE.
UHH... THE LORD'S WORK. WE DID THE LORD'S WORK TOGETHER.

BOB WAS AN ATHEIST.

THAT MADE IT HARD.

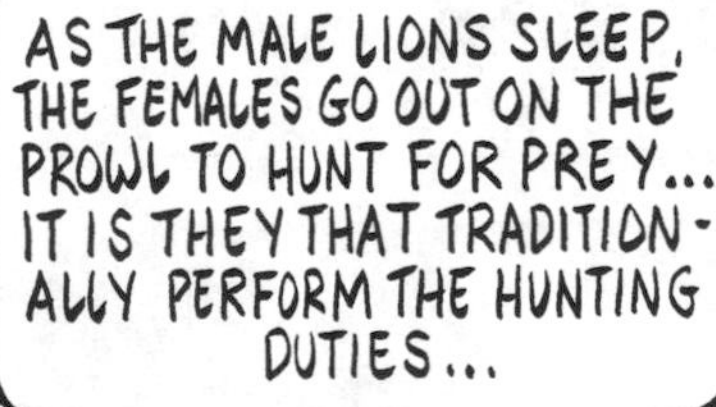
AS THE MALE LIONS SLEEP, THE FEMALES GO OUT ON THE PROWL TO HUNT FOR PREY... IT IS THEY THAT TRADITIONALLY PERFORM THE HUNTING DUTIES...

ONLY AFTER THE PREY IS KILLED DO THE MALES JOIN IN, SHOVING ASIDE THE FEMALES TO GET THE FIRST AND LARGEST SHARE OF THE MEAL... UNFAIR? PERHAPS... BUT THE LAW OF THE JUNGLE.

I'M GONNA KILL YOU, LARRY.

HEY, SIR... IS THAT A CELL PHONE AND A PAGER YOU HAVE CLIPPED TO YOUR BELT?
YEAH. WHY?

BECAUSE IF YOU LOOK UP "TOTAL LOSER GEEK" IN THE DICTIONARY, YOU'LL SEE IT SAYS "MAN WHO CLIPS MULTIPLE ELECTRONIC DEVICES TO HIS BELT."

IS THAT SO?
TAKE IT EASY, SIR. IT'S ONLY A COMIC STRIP.
WE SHOULD GO NOW, RAT.

WHAT ARE YOU DOING, RAT?
I JUST FINISHED WRITING A BOOK.

WHAT'S IT CALLED?
"WHAT MEN WANT."

HOW LONG IS IT?
A PAGE.

IT WOULDA BEEN UNDER A SENTENCE, BUT I FIGURED I'D THROW IN A PARAGRAPH ABOUT BEER.

DO YOU THINK THE WORLD IS FUNDAMENTALLY JUST?
FUNDAMENTALLY JUST WHAT?

JUST FUNDAMENTALLY JUST.

PLEASE STOP MESSING WITH MY MIND.

Okay, zeeba neighba... You is hoomiliate me in front of family for last time... Ees time for you die.
1/27

I SEE.
Oh, you sees, does you? Well, you leesten me. Today you life over. You hear? Over.

YEAH, WELL IT'S LIKE THAT OLD SAYING, ISN'T IT?... IT AIN'T OVER 'TIL THE FAT LADY SINGS.

WHAT ARE YOU WAITING FOR, LARRY? ARE YOU JUST GONNA LET HIM TAUNT YOU LIKE THAT?!

Me was hoping you know a few tunes.

Mebbe not.

I GOT A JOB WRITING SLOGANS THAT PROMOTE BETTER TREATMENT OF SHORT PEOPLE... THEY FACE A LOT OF DISCRIMINATION, YOU KNOW.
THAT'S WONDERFUL... LET ME HEAR ONE.
BEER

"YES, WE MAY BE REALLY TINY, BUT DON'T KICK US IN THE HEINIE."
BEER

1/28
WHY DO YOU ALWAYS LOOK AT ME LIKE THAT?
BEER

WHAT ARE YOU DOING, RAT?
I GOT A JOB MAKING POSTERS THAT PROMOTE BETTER TREATMENT OF SHORT PEOPLE... HERE, HAVE A LOOK AT ONE I JUST DID...

Be nice to us.
1/29

THAT'S A GARDEN GNOME.
IS THERE A DIFFERENCE?

HEY, LOOK, ZEBRA... MINIATURE GOLF.... I'VE NEVER PLAYED BEFORE.
OH, IT'S REAL FUN, PIG... YOU JUST PUTT THE BALL THROUGH CASTLES AND WINDMILLS AND—
MINIATURE GOLF

@#☆@ IT, BOB... I WAS DOING FINE UNTIL THE PAR FIVE NINTH... @#☆@ THAT STUPID HOLE...

OH, GREAT... JUST WHAT I NEED TO CAP OFF MY DAY... A GIANT @##@☆@# PIG IN THE PARKING LOT.
1/30

MAYBE WE SHOULD GO HOME.
OKAY.

WHAT ARE YOU DOING, RAT?
I HAVE WRAPPED MY BODY IN BUBBLEWRAP TO INSULATE MYSELF FROM A WORLD FILLED WITH IDIOTS.

POP POP POP POP POP
1/31

IT'S IRRESISTIBLE.

WHAT HAPPENED TO OUR STUPID GARDEN SHED? IT LOOKS LIKE IT EXPLODED.
I THINK IT WAS THOSE BUNNIES YOU TRIED TO POISON...YOU KNOW, THE ONES WHO ATE YOUR GARDEN?
2/1

WHAT MAKES YOU THINK A BUNCH OF STUPID BUNNIES COULD POSSIBLY BLOW UP OUR GARDEN SHED?
THE VIDEOTAPE THEY SENT.

GREETINGS, GREAT SATAN.

Dear Abby,
I'm a loser.
2/2

Help.

I LIKE TO GET STRAIGHT TO THE POINT.

Angry Bob was angry.
TYPE TYPE

"I will fly a kite," he said. "Flying a kite makes people happy."
TYPITY TYPE

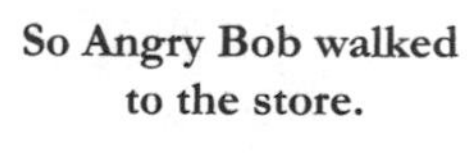

So Angry Bob walked to the store.
TYPE TYPE
TYPE TYPE

"Hello," he said to the man at the store, "I would like to purchase a kite."
TYPE
TYPE

"I am sorry," said the man, "but I am out of kites. Perhaps you'd like a couch."
TYPE TYPE

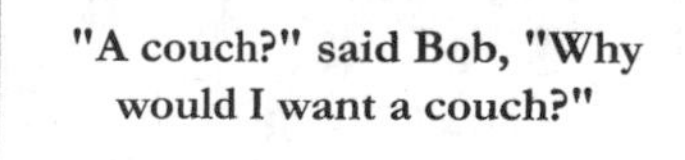

"A couch?" said Bob, "Why would I want a couch?"
TYPITY TYPITY
TYPE

"Because couches are nice," said the man, "And they make people happy."
TYPE TYPE TYPE

Convinced, Bob bought a couch and carried it from the store over his head.
TYPE TYPE

Arriving at a field, he paused. "The man was correct," thought Bob, "This couch will bring me happiness." And for the first time in his 39 years, Bob smiled.
TYPITY TIPPITY

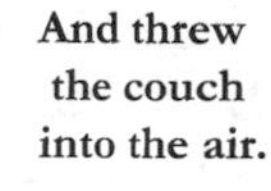

And threw the couch into the air.
TYPE TAP TAP

It did not fly.
TYPE
TYPE TYPE

Bob was crushed like a soft biscuit.
TYPE TYPE

ALWAYS READ THE USER'S MANUAL.

HEY, WHATSA MATTER WITH YOU? IT'S ALMOST NOON.
I WOKE UP DEPRESSED. I'M KINDA HOPING THAT IF I LAY REAL STILL, THE DAY WON'T NOTICE AND I CAN JUST TRY AGAIN TOMORROW.

YOU STUPID PIG. YOU CAN'T DO THAT. WE ALL HAVE TO FACE THE DAY. YOU GET OUTSIDE AND FACE THE DAY!

HI, MOM... NO, PIG'S NOT HERE YET.... HOW SHOULD I KNOW WHY HE'S LATE? BUT I'LL TELL YOU THIS... I'M SICK OF IT.
I'M SICK OF HIS LAZINESS. I'M SICK OF HIS STRANGENESS. I'M SICK OF HIS STUPID EXCUSES.

I GOT HERE AS FAST AS I COULD.

Hullooo zeeba neighba.. Leesten.. What you tink of statue crocs make? Ees called 'Meemorial to Bob.'
WHO'S BOB?

Bob ees a croc who ees close to death.
WHAT'S HE DYING OF?

Ceement.
Can't... breafe... Peese... save....

BEHOLD! MY LATEST CREATION... THE SMART CARD!
WHAT IS IT?

WHEN A DUMB GUY DISAGREES WITH YOU, YOU PULL OUT THE SMART CARD. IT MEANS "I'M SMART. YOU'RE NOT. PLEASE BE QUIET NOW."
OH, GEE... THAT'S JUST SILLY. I MEAN—
2/7

SHHHHHHHHHHHH....

WHAT ARE YOU DOING, RAT?
I AM BONO, ROCK STAR EXTRAORDINAIRE... AND THIS IS MY MANAGER.
YO, BABE.
2/8

YOU'RE NOT BONO... AND YOU CAN'T GO AROUND PRETENDING YOU ARE.
FINE...I SHALL PICK A NEW NAME.... MANAGER, WRITE SOME NEW NAMES...

SCRIBBLE SCRIBBLE

I WILL NOT BE CALLED "BEANO."

IS RAT STILL GOING AROUND PRETENDING HE'S BONO?
YEAH, BUT NOW HE'S GONNA CHANGE HIS NAME TO 'BEANO.'
2/9

I THOUGHT HE HATED THAT NAME.
HE DID, BUT NOW HE'S THINKING THAT WITH A NAME LIKE 'BEANO,' THERE MIGHT BE SOME COMMERCIAL OPPORTUNITIES.

♫ I WANT TO RUUUUN ♫
♪ I WANT TO HIIIIDE ♪
♫ I WANT TO BREAK DOWN THE GAS I'M HOLDING INSIDE... ♫

Zeeba neighba! Me is fall down! Break leg! Help!
FAT CHANCE.. THE SECOND I DID THAT, YOUR BUDDY LARRY WOULD JUMP OUT OF THAT BUSH AND KILL ME.

Ohh, dat not true, Meester Zeeba.
LISTEN, YOUR PAL LARRY HAS THE MIND OF A LITTLE KID.. ALL I HAVE TO DO IS CALL OUT HIS NAME AND HE'LL POP OUT... WATCH...

COME OUT OF THAT BUSH LARRY!
2/10

Ooooooh... You so smart, Meester Zeeba.. HAHAHA See, what me tell yous? No Larry.
SIMON SAYS COME OUT OF THAT BUSH, LARRY!

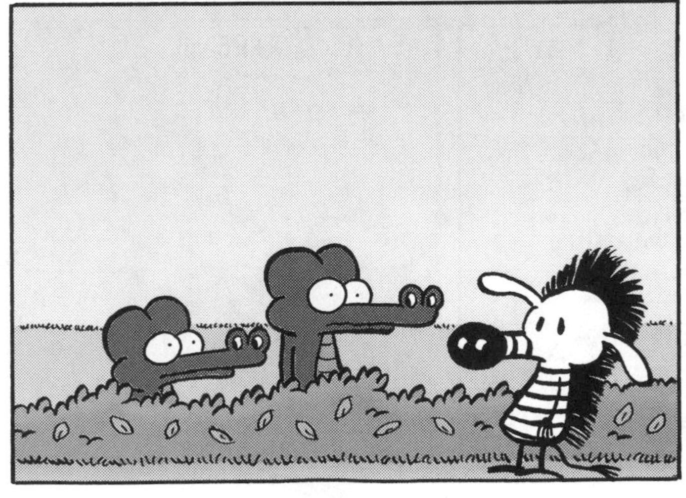

Simon says you beeg fat idiot, Larry.
Simon no say dat, Bob.

Dear Pig,
It's me, your chained-up dog buddy, Andy. I'm writing to give you some good news...

I GOT A GIRLFRIEND!

Although the situation is less than ideal.

2/11

HOLD ME HOLD ME HOLD ME HOLD ME HOLD ME HOLD ME HOLD ME HOLD ME HOLD ME HOLD ME HOLD ME HOLD ME

I CAN'T I CAN'T I CAN'T I CAN'T I CAN'T I CAN'T I CAN'T I CAN'T I CAN'T I CAN'T I CAN'T I CAN'T
2/12

CURSE THESE LONG-DISTANCE RELATIONSHIPS.

OH, OLIVE.. I LOVE YOU.. BUT I SO WANT TO HOLD YOU.
OH, ANDY, ME TOO... BUT WHAT'S IMPORTANT IS HOW WE FEEL ABOUT EACH OTHER...OUR EMOTIONAL INTIMACY...THAT'S EVEN BETTER THAN TOUCHING.
2/13

YOU'RE NUTS.

WHAT ARE YOU DOING, LI'L GUARD DUCK?
I'M STANDING ON THE CRATE O' SADNESS.
Crate O' Sadness

WHY?
BECAUSE MAURA, THE DUCK I LOVED, FLEW SOUTH OVER A YEAR AGO AND NEVER RETURNED.
Crate O' Sadness

SO YOU STAND ON A CRATE?
YES..IT'S WHERE YOU STAND WHEN YOUR DREAMS DON'T COME TRUE.
Crate O' Sadness
2/14

THIS COULD GET CROWDED.
Crate O' Sadness

WHAT ARE YOU DOING, PIG?
I'M SAD TODAY. SO I WAS HOPING IF I ASKED PEOPLE TO SAY WONDERFUL THINGS ABOUT ME, IT MIGHT MAKE ME FEEL UNSAD.
Say wunderfull things about me

YOU STUPID PIG! THERE'S NOTHING WONDERFUL ABOUT A GUY WHO GOES AROUND BEGGING FOR COMPLIMENTS. IT'S PATHETIC! NO ONE'S GONNA HAVE ANYTHING TO SAY.
Say wunderfull things about me
2/15

Say wunderfull things about me
Lying O.K

I'VE CONCLUDED THAT EVERY SINGLE GYM HAS ONE SMELLY GUY WHO DOESN'T SEEM TO KNOW HE'S SMELLY BECAUSE NO ONE WANTS TO TELL HIM.
SO?
2/16

SO NOW THERE'S "SMELLY GUY AWAY!"... FOR JUST $9.99, I WILL WRITE A LETTER TO THAT INDIVIDUAL TACTFULLY APPRISING HIM OF THE SITUATION...HERE, READ A SAMPLE....

Dude, You stink.
I MUST HAVE MISSED THE 'TACTFUL' PART.
IT'S ALL IN THE "DUDE."